"In The Creator and the Cosmos, *D~~r~~ ... ~~r~~ent
cosmological discoveries. Thinking read~~er~~ ... ill
find an accurate presentation of astroph~~y~~ ... ~~y~~
this current research clearly indicates th~~e~~ ... eris-
tics fine-tuned for our life. Though many ... ~~logical~~ conclusion,
the Creator implied by the scientific evidence is exactly consistent with the God
revealed in the Bible."*

Kyle M. Cudworth, Ph.D.
Yerkes Observatory
University of Chicago
Chicago, Illinois

*"A compelling summary of scientific evidence that supports belief in God and the Word
of God, written on a level even the nontechnically trained layperson can understand."*

Walter L. Bradley, Ph.D.
Professor and head of the department of mechanical engineering
Texas A & M University
College Station, Texas

*"*The Creator and the Cosmos *constitutes a remarkable journey through the most
recent scientific findings, providing overwhelming support for design in our universe.
It should prove extremely helpful to those harboring any doubts as to the reliability of
the Bible.*

*"Dr. Ross has documented the evidence for design in our universe in such a thor-
ough yet readable style that it will prove to be of great value both to the science student
as well as the interested layperson."*

David H. Rogstad, Ph.D.
Physicist
Caltech Jet Propulsion Laboratory
Pasadena, California

*"Few eternal themes intrigue individuals—believers and nonbelievers alike—more
than the mystery of creation and the Being of an eternal God. Dr. Hugh Ross, a highly
qualified and gifted cosmologist (a student of the universe) and astronomer/scientist
gives us in this magnificent book irrefutable evidences of God's present and powerful
working in His created universe. Most helpfully it is written in language readily
understandable by those of us who are lay people in the field of astrophysics. This is
must reading for the seeking mind and heart."*

Ted W. Engstrom
President Emeritus
World Vision
Monrovia, California

*"Currently, it is fashionable to believe that the deliverance of science, one and all, are
either hostile or simply irrelevant to the propositions of theology. For some time now,
Hugh Ross has been one of America's leading thinkers who has steadfastly refuted this
claim with hard thinking and up-to-date scientific information. In* The Creator and the
Cosmos *we have a treasure chest containing his most recent work, abreast of the latest
findings of science, and packaged in an accessible form for a general audience. This book
should be in the hands of every serious Christian who thinks about science and the
Christian faith, and it should be given to interested inquirers outside the faith."*

J. P. Moreland, Ph.D.
Professor and director of the Talbot M.A. in philosophy and ethics
Talbot School of Theology, Biola University
La Mirada, California

"Early in this century philosophy rapidly descended down the black hole of logical positivism where God was seemingly erased from the universe. Few could have imagined that by the end of this century breakthroughs in science—quantum mechanics and astrophysics—would ascend out of this abyss to posit the existence of God in the magnificent and endless cathedral of the cosmos. With admirable lucidity, Dr. Hugh Ross navigates through breathtaking panoramas of scientific evidence upon which he builds a compounding case for the biblical world view. With the integrity and credibility of the devoted scientist, he handles a broad range of considerations, giving us invaluable apologetic material—from the design argument, probability, to the facts of physics—that bears witness to the existence of a Creator who is personal and transcendent, whom we can glimpse with a new awe."

Tal Brooke
Author of When the World Will Be as One
President of Spiritual Counterfeits Project
Berkeley, California

THE CREATOR AND THE COSMOS

HOW THE GREATEST SCIENTIFIC DISCOVERIES OF THE CENTURY REVEAL GOD

HUGH ROSS, Ph.D.

NAVPRESS
BRINGING TRUTH TO LIFE
NavPress Publishing Group
P.O. Box 35001, Colorado Springs, Colorado 80935

The Navigators is an international Christian organization. Our mission is to reach, disciple, and equip people to know Christ and to make Him known through successive generations. We envision multitudes of diverse people in the United States and every other nation who have a passionate love for Christ, live a lifestyle of sharing Christ's love, and multiply spiritual laborers among those without Christ.

NavPress is the publishing ministry of The Navigators. NavPress publications help believers learn biblical truth and apply what they learn to their lives and ministries. Our mission is to stimulate spiritual formation among our readers.

© 1993 by Reasons To Believe
Revised edition © 1995
Library of Congress Catalog Card Number: 92-64094
ISBN 08910-97007

Photograph: © Stock Imagery

Ross, Hugh (Hugh Norman), 1945-
        The creator and the cosmos : how the greatest
    scientific discoveries of the century reveal God /
    Hugh Ross.
        p.   cm.
    Includes bibliographical references and index.
    ISBN 0-89109-700-7
    1. Creation.   2. Anthropic principle.   3. God—Proof,
    Cosmological.   I. Title.
    BS651.R76   1993
    231.7'65—dc20   92-64094
                                                         CIP

Printed in the United States of America

4 5 6 7 8 9 10 11 12 13 14 15 16 17 18/99 98

CONTENTS

List of Figures and Tables   6

Preface to the Second Edition   7

Acknowledgments   8

1. The Awe-Inspiring Night Sky   9

2. My Skeptical Inquiry   13

3. The Discovery of the Century   19

4. The Matter Mystery   31

5. The Beautiful Fit   35

6. Einstein's Challenge   49

7. Closing Loopholes: Round One   57

8. Closing Loopholes: Round Two   63

9. Science Discovers Time Before Time   71

10. A God Outside of Time, But Knowable   77

11. A Brief Look at *A Brief History of Time*   87

12. A Modern-Day Goliath   95

13. The Divine Watchmaker   105

14. A "Just Right" Universe   111

15. Earth: The Place for Life   131

16. Building Life   147

17. Extra-Dimensional Power   157

18. The Point   163

Notes   167

Name Index   183

Subject Index   185

LIST OF FIGURES
AND TABLES

Figures
3.1 The Cosmic Background Explorer (COBE) Satellite   21
3.2 COBE's First Measurements of the Spectrum of the Cosmic Background Radiation at the North Galactic Pole of the Heavens   23
3.3 Microwave Map of the Whole Sky Made from One Year of Data Taken by COBE's Differential Microwave Radiameters   26
3.4 The Latest COBE Satellite Results of the Spectrum of the Cosmic Background Radiation   27
5.1 Hubble Space Telescope Being Launched from NASA's Space Shuttle   39
5.2 Gravitational Effect of the "Lens," the Intervening Galaxies and Galaxy Clusters, on the Light from Distant Quasars and Galaxies   41
6.1 The Principle of Invariance   51
6.2 Hubble's Original Velocity-Distance Relation   53
6.3 Einstein and Hubble   55
7.1 Big Bang Growth Versus Steady State Growth   59
8.1 The Infinitely Oscillating Universe Model   64
8.2 Thermodynamic Dissipation Within an Oscillating Universe   65
9.1 Binary Pulsar   74
10.1 God's Time Frame Relative to Our Time Frame   81
12.1 Quantum Tunneling   96
16.1 An Analogy for Some of the Steps Needed in the Assembly of Life Molecules   150

Tables
4.1 Exotic Matter Candidates   32
8.1 Mechanical Efficiencies of Some Common Systems   67
10.1 Some Bible Verses Teaching God's Extra-Dimensional Capacities   78
14.1 Evidence for the Fine Tuning of the Universe   118
15.1 Evidence for the Design of the Galaxy-Sun-Earth-Moon System for Life Support   138
15.2 An Estimate of the Probability for Attaining the Necessary Parameters for Life Support   143

PREFACE TO
THE SECOND EDITION

Since publication of *The Creator and the Cosmos,* first edition, scientists have made many more discoveries that substantially strengthen the evidence for the God of the Bible. This new edition incorporates twenty-one of these latest discoveries.

In response to the new *and* older scientific evidences, non-theistic scholars have developed three more arguments to avoid God. Their arguments are presented and their fallacies exposed.

Several more leading astrophysicists have joined their peers in commenting on the latest astronomical discoveries and the theistic implications. Their comments have been added.

Over a hundred suggestions offered by readers of the first edition have been incorporated to make the text more specific, more complete, and more understandable. In particular, I have added new explanations of exotic, dark, and missing matter, descriptions of new experimental results showing why a cosmic collapse is highly improbable, and definitions for the four kinds of *nothing* physicists discuss. I trust you will find *something* here to further inspire and strengthen your faith in our awesome Creator.

ACKNOWLEDGMENTS

My wife, Kathy, deserves the most credit for this book's timely publication. Her support and encouragement during times of stress and deadlines for this and other projects allowed me to persevere. In addition to doing the majority of the editing and rewriting, she spent many hours discussing with me the points of this book and helping me to communicate them more clearly.

Janet Kobobel, the director of publications for Reasons To Believe, was also a major contributor to the editing and rewriting. Several of the word pictures used to clarify technical points are hers. She also kept us coordinated and handled communications with the publisher, artists, and others.

I benefited greatly from discussions with Drs. David and Lynn Carta, Sam Conner, and Allan Sandage. And all of them provided me with important research papers and references. Mal Scharer spent many hours in various libraries hunting down additional references.

Sheila Cherney obtained all of the photographs and permissions. Patty Bradbury provided extra care for my sons, Joel and David, enabling Kathy and me to work as a team. Thanks to Dr. John Rowe, the office staff, and the apologetics hotline volunteers of Reasons To Believe, I was able to delegate many of my normal responsibilities to them and concentrate on this book.

Lastly, I want to thank Lauren Libby and Dr. Jerry White of The Navigators and Steve Webb of NavPress for their enthusiasm and support of this project.

CHAPTER ONE

THE AWE-INSPIRING NIGHT SKY

When I was eight, I started saving to buy a telescope. It took several years, but finally I pulled together enough coins to purchase the optics. With my father's help, I designed and built a mount and, at last, peered through the telescope to the heavens above.

I was stunned. I had never seen anything so beautiful, so awesome. The spectacle was too good not to share. I carried my instrument from the back yard to the front so I could invite my neighbors to join me. But no invitation was necessary. No sooner had I planted my telescope on the sidewalk than an enthusiastic crowd formed, a crowd that stayed late into the night.

That evening I began to realize many people, maybe all people, are fascinated with the starry hosts. I once thought that the sheer immensity of the heavens was responsible for that fascination. That's part of it, but there's more. There's the mystery of what's really out there, what those specks of light may be, the mystery of how they all got there and of what lies above and beyond. Gazing at the night sky seems to raise profound questions not only about the universe but also about ourselves.

The Universe and You
Cosmology is the study of the universe as a whole—its structure, origin, and development. It's not a subject just for ivory tower academics. Cosmology is for everyone.

In the words of historian, economist, and college president Dr. George Roche, "It really does matter, and matter very much, how we think about the cosmos."[1] Roche's point is that our concept of the universe shapes our world view, our philosophy of life, and thus our daily decisions and actions.

For example, if the universe is not created or is in some manner accidental, then it has no objective meaning, and consequently, life, including human life, has no meaning. A mechanical chain of events determines everything. Morality and religion may be temporarily useful but are ultimately irrelevant. The Universe (capital U) is ultimate reality.

On the other hand, if the universe is created, then there must be reality beyond the confines of the universe. The Creator is that ultimate reality and wields authority over all else. The Creator is the source of life and establishes its meaning and purpose. The Creator's personality defines personality. The Creator's character defines morality.

Thus, to study the origin and development of the universe is, in a sense, to investigate the basis for any meaning and purpose to life. Cosmology has deep theological and philosophical ramifications.

Unfortunately, many researchers refuse to acknowledge this connection. In the name of objectivity, they gather and examine data through a special pair of glasses, the "God-is-not-necessary-to-explain-anything" glasses. It's tough for them to admit that such lenses represent their theological position, their personal faith. I've also met researchers who read the universe through the "God-is-whoever-or-whatever-I-choose" glasses.

Though no one is perfectly objective, some researchers are willing to gather and integrate the data to see which theory of origins is most consistent with the facts—whatever that theory may say about the necessity and characteristics of an Originator.

Cosmological Chauvinism

Because cosmology probes such weighty and personal matters, it has evoked possessiveness and competition. This is perhaps more evident today than ever. Three groups vie for supreme authority on the subject: scientists, theologians, and philosophers.

The chauvinism of scientists is exemplified by a pep talk I heard in my undergraduate days at the University of British Columbia. "Not only can a good physicist do physics better than anyone else," said the professor, "he can do anything better than anyone else." He expressed the belief that science training is essential for grappling with the challenges of modern life. In a graduate course on relativity, my professor lamented theologians' past meddling in cosmology. "Today," he boasted, "we have been able to scare most of the ministers out of cosmology with a straightforward application of tensor calculus."[2]

At a meeting of philosophers, I heard a distinguished speaker commiserate with his peers over scientists' bungling intrusion into cosmology. "Even the best physicists," he said, "are lousy philosophers."

At a theology colloquium, I heard from the podium that theologians alone have the right to interpret all science since they are trained in the mother of the sciences, theology. The speaker ended on a dramatic note: "Scientists have only observations. We have revelation!"

Cosmological chauvinism is not simply a manifestation of academic pride. It reflects decades of increasing specialization in education. Universities long ago dropped theology from their science curriculum. Few, if any, seminaries draw students with a background in science. Philosophy students may touch upon theology and science, but usually not in depth. Theology and philosophy students may study the history of their disciplines, science students rarely do.

The inevitable fruits of such specialization are polarization, conflict, and misunderstanding, not to mention neglect of the ordinary people whose tax dollars support much of the research in cosmology. I realize that specialization is necessary to push forward the frontiers of knowledge, but imagine how much more efficiently and effectively we could learn about reality if we were to take an interdisciplinary approach, giving adequate attention to historical context.

If specialists will stop intimidating each other and lay people and start dialoguing in understandable terms, anyone who wants to can explore and integrate the facts about our universe. Then we all, novices included, can enrich our understanding of the meaning and purpose for the universe, for life, for humanity, and for every person.

CHAPTER TWO

MY SKEPTICAL INQUIRY

My own thinking about the meaning of life began with my wonderment about the cosmos. I was born shortly after World War II in Montreal, Canada. My father was a self-taught engineer, and my mother a nurse. Before and during my early years my father founded and built up a successful hydraulics engineering business. The company's rapid financial growth proved too great a temptation for Dad's financial partner, who one day withdrew all the funds and vanished. With his last few dollars, my dad brought my mother, my two sisters, and me to Vancouver, British Columbia. The neighborhood in which we settled was poor but culturally diverse. Our neighbors were mostly refugees from eastern Europe and Asia—people who, like my parents, had tasted success but either lost it or left it for survival's sake.

Are Stars Hot?

My parents say they could see in me an intense curiosity about nature from the time I started to talk. I recall one starlit evening when I was seven, walking along the sidewalk with my parents and asking them if the stars are hot. They assured me that they are very hot. When I asked them why, they suggested I go to the library. They knew I would.

My elementary school library was well stocked with books on astronomy. As I read, I was amazed to discover just how hot the stars are and what makes them burn so brightly. I found out that our galaxy contains a hundred billion suns and that our universe holds more than a hundred billion galaxies. I was astonished by the immensity of it all. I was compelled to find out everything I could about it.

In my eighth year I read every book on physics and astronomy

I could find in our school library. The next year I began to do the same in the children's section of the Vancouver Public Library.

By that time I knew I wanted to be an astronomer. Many of my friends also were reading incessantly and choosing career directions. We didn't think of ourselves as precocious. The nonstop rainfall in Vancouver encouraged a lot of indoor activity and provided plenty of time to think.

At age ten I had exhausted the science resources of the children's and youth sections of the Vancouver Public Library and was granted a pass to the adult section. A few years later I was given access to the library of the University of British Columbia. By the time I was sixteen, I was presenting public lectures on astronomy and at seventeen won the British Columbia Science Fair for my project on variable stars. Also at seventeen I became the director of observations for the Vancouver branch of the Royal Astronomical Society of Canada (an organization of primarily amateur astronomers). I felt glad to have found so early in life a pursuit I loved.

Who Did All This?

Even as a child I always felt a sense of awe concerning nature. Its beauty and harmony, combined with its staggering complexity, left me wondering who or what could be responsible for it all.

By age fifteen, I came to understand that some form of the big bang theory provided the only reasonable explanation for the universe. If the universe arose out of a big bang, it must have had a beginning. If it had a beginning, it must have a Beginner.

From that point on, I never doubted God's existence. But, like the astronomers whose books I read, I presumed that the Beginner was distant and noncommunicative. Surely, I reasoned, a God who built a universe of more than ten-billion-trillion stars would not concern Himself with events on an insignificant speck of dust we call Earth.

Ruling Out Holy Books

My high school history studies bothered me because they showed me that the peoples of the world typically take their religions seriously. Knowing that the European philosophers of the Enlightenment largely discounted religion, I first looked for insight from their works. What I discovered, however, were circular arguments, inconsistencies, contradictions, and evasions. I began to appreciate nature all the more, for it never presented me with such twists.

Just to be fair and not to build a case on second-hand resources, I determined to investigate for myself the holy books of the world's major religions. I figured if God, the Creator, was speaking through any of these books (I presumed He was not), then the communication would be noticeably distinct from what human beings write. I reasoned that if humans invented a religion, their message would contain errors and inconsistencies, but if the Creator communicated, His message would reflect His supernature. It would be consistent like nature is. I chose history and science as good ways to test the revelations on which various religions are based.

In the first several holy books I examined, my initial hunch was confirmed. I found statements clearly at odds with established history and science (see chapter 8, page 69, for an example). I also noted a writing style perhaps best described as esoteric, mysterious, and vague. My great frustration was having to read so much in these books to find something stated specifically enough to be tested. The sophistry and the incongruity with established facts seemed opposite to the Creator's character as suggested to me by nature.

A Word from God?

I was getting a little smug until I picked up a Bible I had received (but not read) from the Gideons at my public school. The book's distinctives struck me immediately. It was simple, direct, and specific. I was amazed with the quantity of historical and scientific references and with the detail in them.

It took me a whole evening just to investigate the first chapter. Instead of another bizarre creation myth, here was a journal-like record of the earth's initial conditions—correctly described from the standpoint of astrophysics and geophysics—followed by a summary of the sequence of changes through which Earth came to be inhabited by living things and ultimately by humans. The account was simple, elegant, and scientifically accurate. From what I understood to be the stated viewpoint of an observer on Earth's surface, both the order and the description of creation events perfectly matched the established record of nature. I was amazed.

That night I committed myself to spend at least an hour a day going through the Bible to test the accuracy of all its statements on science, geography, and history. I expected this study to take about four weeks. Instead, there was so much to check it took me eighteen months.

At the end of the eighteen months, I had to admit to myself that I had been unsuccessful in finding a single provable error or contradiction. This is not to say that there were not any passages in the Bible I did not understand or problems that I could not resolve. The problems and passages I couldn't yet understand didn't discourage me, however, for I faced the same kinds of things in the record of nature. But, just as with the record of nature, I was impressed with how much could be understood and resolved.

I was now convinced that the Bible was supernaturally accurate and thus supernaturally inspired. Its perfection could come only from the Creator Himself. I also recognized that the Bible stood alone in revealing God and His dealings with humans from a perspective that demanded more than just the dimensions we mortals can experience (length, width, height, and time). Since humans cannot visualize phenomena in dimensions they cannot experience, finding these ideas in the Bible also argued for a superhuman author.

As a final exercise, I mathematically determined that the Bible was more reliable by far than some of the laws of physics. For example, I knew from studying physics there is roughly a one in 10^{80} (that's the number one with eighty zeros following) chance of a sudden reversal in the second law of thermodynamics. But I had calculated (with the help of skeptical friends) the probability of the chance fulfillment of thirteen Bible predictions about specific people and their specific actions. My conservative estimate showed less than one chance in 10^{138} that such predictions could come true without supernatural intervention.[1] That meant the Bible was 10^{58} times more reliable than the second law of thermodynamics on just this one set of predictions.

Acknowledging that my life depended moment by moment on the reliability of the second law of thermodynamics, I saw that my only rational option was to trust in the Bible's Inspirer to at least the same degree as I relied on the laws of physics. I realized, too, what a self-sufficient young man I had been. After a long evening of studying the salvation passages in the New Testament, I humbled myself before God, asking Him to forgive me of my self-exaltation and all the offenses resulting from it, and committed myself to follow His directives for my life. At 1:06 in the morning I signed my name on the back page of my Gideon Bible, stating that I had received Christ as my Lord and Savior.[2]

New Evidences

All of the scientific and historical evidences I had collected deeply rooted my confidence in the veracity of the Bible and convinced me that the Creator had indeed communicated through this holy book. I went on to become an astronomer, and my investigations into both the cosmos and the Bible have shown me a more wondrous, personal God behind nature than I could ever have imagined.

Through the years, new evidences have consistently arisen in various fields of science, making the case for Christianity even stronger. By 1986, several breakthrough discoveries uncovered proofs for the God of the Bible so convincing that together with others I formed an organization, Reasons To Believe, to communicate these new evidences to as many people as possible.

Now, six years later, an even more dramatic set of scientific discoveries has come. One of them has been called the greatest discovery of the century. Secular scientists have reported to the media that these new findings reveal the face of God more clearly than ever. The following chapter explores how and why normally reserved scientists have been moved to speak in such ecstatic terms.

CHAPTER THREE

THE DISCOVERY
OF THE CENTURY

On April 24, 1992, newspapers around the world heralded a breakthrough by an American research team. The discovery made the front-page headlines of *The London Times* for five consecutive days. American TV networks gave the story as much as forty minutes of prime-time news coverage.

Reactions by Scientists

What was all the fuss about? A team of astrophysicists had reported the latest findings from the Cosmic Background Explorer (COBE) satellite—stunning confirmation of the hot big bang creation event.

Scientists extolled the event with superlatives. Carlos Frenk, of Britain's Durham University, exclaimed, "[It's] the most exciting thing that's happened in my life as a cosmologist."[1] Cambridge University's Lucasian professor of mathematics, Stephen Hawking, known for understatement, said, "It is the discovery of the century, if not of all time."[2] Michael Turner, astrophysicist with the University of Chicago and Fermilab, termed the discovery "unbelievably important. . . . The significance of this cannot be overstated. They have found the Holy Grail of cosmology."[3]

Turner's metaphor echoed a familiar theme. George Smoot, University of California at Berkeley astronomer and project leader for the COBE satellite, declared, "What we have found is evidence for the birth of the universe."[4] He added, "It's like looking at God."[5]

Theistic pronouncements abounded. According to science historian Frederic B. Burnham, the community of scientists was prepared to consider the idea that God created the universe "a more respectable hypothesis today than at any time in the last hundred years."[6] Ted Koppel on ABC's "Nightline" began his interview of an astronomer and a physicist by quoting the first two verses of Genesis. The physicist immediately added verse three as also germane to the discovery.

Astronomers who do not draw theistic or deistic conclusions are becoming rare, and even the few dissenters hint that the tide is against them. Geoffrey Burbidge, of the University of California at San Diego, complains that his fellow astronomers are rushing off to join "the First Church of Christ of the Big Bang."[7]

Proofs of the Big Bang

All this excitement was generated because findings from the COBE satellite helped solve a haunting mystery of the big bang model for the origin and development of the universe, thus confirming that model (actually a set of models) and refining it.

Basically the hot big bang model says that the entire physical universe—all the matter and energy, and even the four dimensions of space and time—burst forth from a state of infinite, or near infinite, density, temperature, and pressure. The universe expanded from a volume very much smaller than the period at the end of this sentence, and it continues to expand.

Before April 1992, astrophysicists knew a great deal about how the universe began. Only one small but important component was missing. It was as if they knew how the machine was assembled and how it worked except for one part. They knew what that part should look like, and they knew approximately where to look for it. The COBE satellite (see figure 3.1, page 21) was designed specifically to find this missing part—namely, the explanation for how galaxies form out of a big bang.

Actually, the entire machine itself and many of its basic components were predicted by physicists working in the early part of the twentieth century. Richard Tolman in 1922 recognized that since the universe is expanding, it must be cooling off from an exceptionally high initial temperature.[8] The laws of thermodynamics say that any expanding system must be cooling simultaneously. George Gamow in 1946 discovered that only a rapid cooling of the cosmos from near infinitely high temperatures could account for how protons and neutrons fused together, forming a universe that today is about 73% hydrogen, 24% helium, and 3% heavier elements.[9]

The Cosmic Oven

Astronomers knew, based on the deductions by Tolman and Gamow, that the universe's beginning and subsequent development resembled a hot kitchen oven. When the door of the oven is opened, heat that was trapped inside escapes. Dissipation of the oven's heat takes place as the heat expands outward from the oven. Radiant energy that was confined to a few cubic feet now spreads throughout the kitchen's several hundred cubic feet. As it does, the oven cavity eventually cools down to the temperature of the room, which is now just a little warmer than it was before.

If one knows the peak temperature of the oven cavity, the volume of that cavity, and the volume of the room throughout which the oven's heat is dissipated, then the amount by which the room will warm up can be determined.

If one were using the opening of the oven door to dry out some wet towels, it would be important to control the temperature of the oven as well as the rate at which the oven disperses its heat to the room.

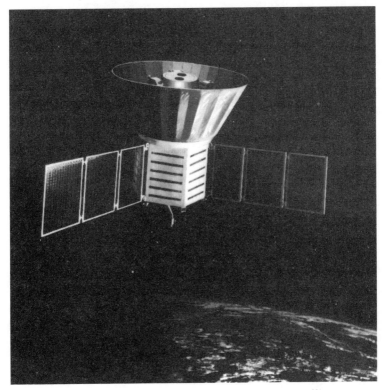

Figure 3.1: The Cosmic Background Explorer (COBE) Satellite
— *Photo courtesy of Jet Propulsion Laboratory, NASA.*

If the oven were too hot, or the dispersion too slow, the towels would scorch. But, if the oven were too cool, or the heat dissipation too rapid (say the room was too large or the towels too far away), the towels would stay wet.

Similarly, if the universe were to expand too slowly, too many of the nucleons (protons and neutrons) would fuse together to form heavier elements. This would result in too few of the lighter elements essential for life chemistry. On the other hand, if the expansion were more rapid, too many of the nucleons would fuse into lighter elements. This would result in too few of the heavier elements essential for life chemistry.

Following this oven analogy, Gamow's research team in 1948 calculated what temperature conditions would be necessary to yield the currently observed abundances of elements. They concluded that a faint glow measuring only about 5° degree Centigrade above absolute zero (that's -273° degree Centigrade or -460° degree Fahrenheit) should be found everywhere throughout the universe.[10]

At the time, such a low temperature was hopelessly beyond the capabilities of telescopes and detectors to measure. But by 1964 Arno Penzias and Robert Wilson put together an instrument that successfully measured at radio wavelengths the cosmic background radiation (i.e., heat) to be at a temperature about 3° degree Celsius above absolute zero.[11] Since that initial discovery, the cosmic background radiation has been measured to much greater accuracy and at many more wavelengths.[12] But at most of the wavelengths the cosmic background radiation remained blocked out by the earth's atmosphere and, therefore, was beyond detection. Only a telescope operating in outer space could see well enough.

First COBE Discovery
The first COBE results, reported in January 1990,[13] showed the universe to match a perfect radiator, dissipating virtually all its available energy (see figure 3.2, page 23). The data showed the background radiation temperature to be very low and smooth. No irregularities in the temperature larger than one part in 10,000 were detected.

This extraordinarily low and smooth temperature in the cosmic background radiation convinced astronomers that the universe must have had an extremely hot beginning about 15 to 20 billion years ago. The finding essentially ruled out many alternative models for the universe's beginning such as the steady state model (see chapter 7). How were scientists able to conclude from these COBE findings a hot and relatively recent beginning for the universe? For some clues, let's return to our analogy of the kitchen oven.

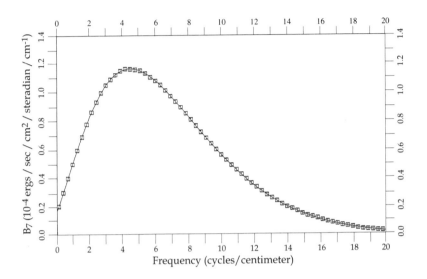

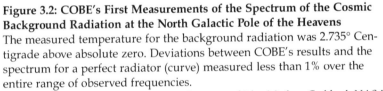

Figure 3.2: COBE's First Measurements of the Spectrum of the Cosmic Background Radiation at the North Galactic Pole of the Heavens
The measured temperature for the background radiation was 2.735° Centigrade above absolute zero. Deviations between COBE's results and the spectrum for a perfect radiator (curve) measured less than 1% over the entire range of observed frequencies.

— Courtesy of John Mather, Goddard, NASA.

Suppose the oven were surrounded by thousands of thermometers, each placed at exactly the same distance from the oven. Suppose also that some time after the oven had been heated, turned off, and its door opened, each thermometer indicated exactly the same temperature. The only possible conclusion we could draw would be that heat flow from the oven cavity to the room totally dominated the normal temperature-disturbing air flows in the room. Such dominance would imply that the original temperature of the oven cavity must have been very much greater than the room's temperature. In addition, if all those thousands of thermometers indicated a very low temperature, we would conclude that considerable time had passed since the opening of the oven door.

The Fantastic Explosion

The temperature measurements from COBE provide convincing evidence of a hot origin for the cosmos some billions of years in the past. Astronomers normally refer to this hot beginning as the big bang for a very good reason.

The cool and uniform temperature of the cosmic background radiation and its close fit to the spectrum of a perfect radiator establishes that the universe has suffered an enormous degradation of energy, typical of a large explosion. Energy degradation is measured by a quantity called entropy. Entropy describes the degree to which energy in a closed system disperses, or radiates (as heat), and thus ceases to be available to perform work. Specific entropy is the measure for a particular system of the amount of entropy per proton.

A burning candle is a good example of a highly entropic system, one that efficiently radiates energy away. It has a specific entropy of about two. Only very hot explosions have much higher specific entropies. The specific entropy of the universe—about one billion—is enormous beyond all comparison. Even supernova explosions, the most entropic (and radiant) of events now occurring in the universe, have specific entropies a hundred times less.

Only a hot big bang could account for such a huge specific entropy for the universe. (Let me be quick to add for those bothered to learn that the universe is so "inefficient" a machine, that only a universe with a huge specific entropy can produce the observed abundances of elements.[14] It can also be shown that if the specific entropy were any greater or any less, stars and planets would never have existed at any time in the universe's history.[15])

Second COBE Discovery

The smoothness of the cosmic background radiation helped confirm a hot big bang beginning for the universe. But it posed a potential problem for a stage of development that scientists estimated would occur roughly a billion years after the creation event. Astronomers knew that the background radiation could not be perfectly smooth. At least some level of non-uniformity in the cosmic background radiation would be necessary to explain the formation of galaxies and clusters of galaxies. The whole range of reasonable theories for how galaxies can come together required temperature fluctuations roughly ten times smaller than what COBE had the capability to detect in 1990. Fortunately, the results announced on April 24, 1992, were between ten and a hundred times more precise than the measurements from 1990.

These newly refined COBE measurements showed irregularities in the background radiation as large as about one part in 100,000,[16] just what astrophysicists thought they would find.[17] That missing piece of the machinery was located exactly where they suspected it might be. What's more, the measurements solved some intriguing mysteries about the piece itself—what it's made of and how it works. They could narrow the galaxy formation theories to those that include both ordinary matter and an amazing component called exotic matter. More on this in chapter 4, "The Matter Mystery."

Confirmations

To be complete I must report that these dramatic COBE results (see figure 3.3, page 26) did meet with some initial challenges from a few astronomers, including Geoffrey Burbidge.[18] But their skepticism seemed unwarranted to other astronomers since the temperature irregularities showed up in the identical locations of the heavens at three different wavelengths of observation.

Within a few months, corroborative evidence began to accumulate. A balloon-borne experiment, making measurements at four different wavelengths that were shorter than the three measured by COBE, showed temperature fluctuations lining up perfectly with those in the COBE maps. Edward Cheng, leader of the experiment, concluded, "With two totally different systems, it's very unlikely that random noise would give rise to the same lumps at the same places in the sky."[19]

Twelve months later, two radiometers operating in Tenerife, Spain, detected actual structure in the cosmic background radiation. Whereas the COBE and balloon measurements were sensitive enough to establish that fluctuations in the cosmic background radiation did indeed exist, they could not delineate with any accuracy the location and size of individual features. This delineation was achieved through fully independent radiometers operating at three different wavelengths, longer than the wavelengths observed by COBE and the balloon-borne instruments. The angular scale (size of the angle in the sky over which measurements were made) was 5.5°. Fluctuation structures as large as ten degrees across were found, and the amplitude of these structures is completely consistent with the earlier statistical detections by COBE and the balloon-borne experiment.[20]

Even more recently, cosmic background radiation fluctuations on angular scales of about 1° were detected. These latest measurements also are consistent with the detections by COBE and the balloon-borne experiment.[21]

Still stronger confirmation comes from a variety of recent detections of exotic matter (see chapter 5, "The Beautiful Fit"). The important point to remember is that galaxy formation no longer casts a shadow of doubt on the big bang scenario.

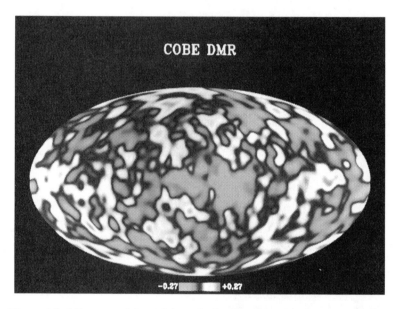

Figure 3.3: Microwave Map of the Whole Sky Made from One Year of Data Taken by COBE's Differential Microwave Radiometers (DMR)
The Milky Way galaxy lies horizontal across the middle of the map. Data from all three DMR wavelengths were used to model and remove emission from our galaxy. This map revealed for the first time temperature fluctuations in the cosmic background radiation. The amplitudes of the fluctuations are consistent with explaining the birth and growth of galaxies using large amounts of exotic matter.
— *Photo courtesy of Jet Propulsion Laboratory, NASA.*

Third COBE Discovery

Deviations between the 1990 COBE results and the spectrum for a perfect radiator measured less than 1% over the entire range of observed frequencies (see figure 3.2, page 23). Data released from the COBE research team (see figure 3.4, page 27) at an American Astronomical Society meeting in January 1993 reduce the deviation to less than 0.03%. The new data also yield the most precise measure to date of the temperature of the cosmic background radiation, 2.726° Kelvin (that is 2.726° Centigrade above absolute zero), a measure that is accurate to within 0.01°K[22] and completely consistent with a recent independent measurement.[23]

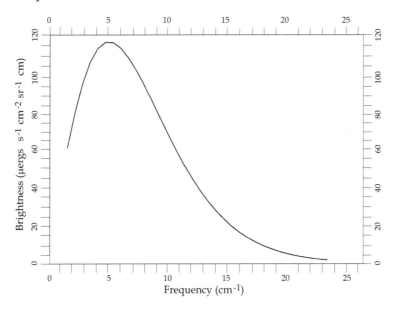

Figure 3.4: The Latest COBE Satellite Results of the Spectrum of the Cosmic Background Radiation
Deviations between COBE's measurements and the spectrum for a perfect radiator (curve) are less than 0.03% over the entire range of observed frequencies. This is the strongest direct evidence to date for a hot big bang creation event.

– Courtesy of John Mather, Goddard, NASA.

Keck Discovery

Let me clarify that the temperature 2.726°K for the cosmic background radiation is for nearby regions of space. Because radiation from great distances takes much longer to reach us, temperatures at such distances reveal the heat of the cosmos at earlier times. If the hot big bang model is correct, observations at great distances should yield significantly higher temperatures for the cosmic background radiation. For this reason, astronomers for many years have desired to measure the cosmic background radiation at great distances.

In September 1994 that desire was fulfilled. The newly opened Keck Telescope, the world's largest optical instrument, enabled astronomers to measure spectral lines of carbon in two gas clouds so distant that their radiation represents an epoch when the universe was about one-fourth its present age. They were able to select lines that would provide a sensitive measure of the temperature of the cosmic background radiation. According to the hot big bang model, the background radiation for the universe at this early epoch should be $7.58°K$. The Keck Telescope observations indicated $7.4\pm0.8°K$.[24] In the words of David Meyer, Northwestern University astrophysicist, these measurements are "strikingly consistent with the Big Bang theory."[25]

Helium and Deuterium in the Early Universe

Another prediction of the big bang theory is that most of the universe's helium and deuterium ("heavy" hydrogen, hydrogen with both a neutron and a proton in its nucleus) are generated within the first four minutes following the creation event. Until recently, astronomers' confirmation of this prediction was limited to measuring the abundance of helium and deuterium in our own galaxy and in a few nearby galaxies, subtracting the quantities arising from other astrophysical sources (primarily stars).[26] But in April and August of 1994, important breakthroughs came. Astronomers measured for the first time the abundance of helium and deuterium in very distant intergalactic gas clouds. Because light takes so long to reach us from these gas clouds, what astronomers see there is the condition of the universe billions of years ago, before any helium or deuterium could be produced or destroyed by sources other than the big bang event. And what did they find? Quantities of helium and deuterium precisely anticipated by big bang nucleosynthesis theory[27] and totally consistent with measurements made in nearby galaxies.[28]

These new results do more than just prove that the universe began with a hot big bang. They tell us which kind of hot big bang. The 1990 results left room for the possibility that the big bang could have been a tightly spaced succession of "little" bangs. The new results rule out that possibility. The universe must have erupted from a single explosive event that by itself accounts for at least 99.97% of the radiant energy in the universe.

With a single explosive creation event accounting for so much of the radiation in the universe, astronomers can conclude that the temperature fluctuations in the cosmic background radiation, not disturbances arising from smaller events, must have transformed the smooth primordial cosmos into today's universe of clumped clusters of galaxies.

CHAPTER FOUR

THE MATTER MYSTERY

Anyone who has worked on machines, from vacuum cleaners to car engines, knows that if a part is needed for the machine to function, it must be the right part, a part manufactured to fit. A Eureka belt will not fix a Hoover vacuum cleaner. A Honda carburetor will not make a Chevy go.

So it is with the big bang and one of its key components, galaxy formation. Astrophysicists are still in the process of narrowing down which big bang model comes closest to accounting for all the observed (and potentially observable) facts about the universe.

One way big bang models differ from one another is in the way they predict the formation of galaxies. Galaxy formation theories once said that the stuff of which the universe is made is ordinary matter only. But these theories did not fit the observations. Others proposed that at least some of another kind of matter, dubbed exotic matter, must be necessary to galaxy formation. By affirming that this exotic matter exists and by determining how much in proportion to ordinary matter, astronomers can narrow down their search for the best (as in, closest to reality) big bang model.

Exotic Versus Ordinary

Decades ago the only kind of matter anyone knew about was ordinary matter. Ordinary matter is the stuff we are used to—matter made up of protons, neutrons, electrons, and other fundamental particles that are detected easily in particle physics experiments. Such matter strongly interacts with radiation.

Exotic matter has the opposite characteristic of ordinary matter. It does not strongly interact with radiation. Particle physicists have classified thirty-six different fundamental particles or massive objects that could fit this description.[1] Since the names of such particles and objects are creeping into popular magazines, a few of the better known examples are listed in table 4.1, along with some basic characteristics. Because of how weakly these particles interact with radiation, however, none has been detected (as yet) in a laboratory experiment.

Table 4.1: Exotic Matter Candidates
These candidates could make up the proportion of the mass of the universe that does not strongly interact with radiation (note: $10^{-5} = .00001$ and $10^6 = 1,000,000$).

Exotic Matter Candidate	Mass Relative to a Proton	Density (number per cm³)	Velocity Profile
axions, majorons	10^{-14}–10^{-10}	10^9	cold
low mass neutrinos	10^{-8}	100	hot
gravitinos	10^{-6}	10	warm
axinos, mirror particles	10^{-6}	10	warm/cold
photinos, higgsinos, gluinos	10^{-1}	10^{-4}	cold
heavy neutrinos	1	10^{-5}	cold
magnetic monopoles	10^{16}	10^{-21}	cold
newtorites	10^{19}	10^{-24}	cold
maximons and pyrgons	10^{19}	10^{-24}	cold
supersymmetric strings	10^{19}	10^{-24}	cold
quark nuggets	10^{39}	10^{-44}	cold
primordial black holes	10^{40}	10^{-45}	cold

As the table shows, exotic matter is strange stuff indeed. It can run the gamut from particles with masses of less than a trillionth of a proton, to particles with masses exceeding a quadrillion protons, to objects as massive as a typical asteroid. More frequently, exotic matter candidates are classified as cold dark matter (particles moving at low velocities), hot dark matter (particles moving at velocities near the speed of light), or warm dark matter (particles moving at intermediate velocities).

Because exotic matter only weakly interacts with radiation, it can function almost independently from radiation. Thus exotic matter could clump while the radiation remains nearly smooth. Then, through the action of gravity (two massive bodies will attract one another whether or not the mass is ordinary, exotic, or a combination of both), the exotic matter could attract ordinary matter to it. In this way, galaxies and galaxy clusters would form without causing huge waves in the background radiation.

Simple and Beautiful

Just prior to 1992, astrophysicists had designed several simple big bang models that included exotic matter. In these models they determined approximately how much exotic matter in relation to ordinary matter would be needed for the galaxies to clump as we observe them today while the background radiation remained relatively smooth. They also calculated how much the temperature of the cosmic background radiation would fluctuate if the proposed quantity of exotic matter were present. On April 24, the radiation ripple measurements announced by George Smoot's team precisely matched the level of fluctuation the astrophysicists had predicted. No wonder elation followed.

The April announcement solved the one critical difficulty of the big bang model: how the galaxies clumped while the background radiation remained so smooth. It is this solution that gave rise to Michael Turner's and others' ecstatic exclamations.

And yet there is more to the Holy Grail than just the discovery of ripples in the cosmic background radiation. In the months surrounding the April 24 announcement came several other enormously significant discoveries. Together these discoveries prove the stability of the big bang model. They also reflect its beauty.

CHAPTER FIVE

THE BEAUTIFUL FIT

Ironically, the April 24 discovery came almost simultaneously with seven other cosmological breakthroughs. Though these other breakthroughs ranked right up there in significance with the radiation ripples, they received barely a peep from the popular press. The only explanation I can offer for this neglect is that these other seven discoveries may be a little more complicated to understand and describe.

Taken together, the eight discoveries provide overwhelming evidence that astronomers and astrophysicists are on the right track in determining that a hot big bang model best describes how the universe came to be—and in concluding that God is the power and intelligence behind it all.

The seven additional discoveries clarify our understanding of galaxy formation. The newfound key to that understanding is exotic matter. Each of the discoveries sheds light on the quantity of exotic matter in the universe, which in turn sheds light on how the universe became clumpy enough for galaxies and clusters of galaxies to form. This accumulation of new findings means that the big bang ripples discovery does not stand on its own. It is solidly supported from many different angles.

Measuring the Amount of Exotic Matter
Rough calculation of the amount of exotic matter from observations of the subtle radiation ripples and from the clumpiness of galaxies provides an indirect measure. It's like determining an elephant's weight from the depth of his footprints in the mud and from the consistency of the mud at the time he walked through it. This calculation is fairly reliable, but the closer we can get to direct measures, such as the elephant's stepping on a scale, the more we can trust it.

And these closer-to-direct measures are what we now have. Between January and June of 1992 astronomers developed and used for the first time seven independent tools to measure the amount of one or both kinds of matter in the universe. They also discovered another contributor to clumpiness, which may slightly affect their measurements. First let's take a look at the eight measuring devices:

1. Deuterium Abundance

Deuterium is heavy hydrogen. A typical hydrogen atom has a single proton; deuterium atoms have a proton plus a neutron. As the universe cools from the creation event, there is a period of only a few seconds when its temperature will be just right for the nuclear fusion of protons and neutrons into deuterium atoms. Because of the brevity of this period, the amount of deuterium will be small. Whatever amount does form will be in direct proportion to the total amount of ordinary matter in the universe. Thus, in measuring the amount of deuterium (relative to the abundances of other elements) in the universe, astronomers can determine the quantity of ordinary matter.

EXOTIC, DARK, AND MISSING MATTER

Luminous stars make up only a tiny fraction of the total mass of the universe. The rest is "dark matter." Because astronomers are certain that this dark matter exists, in spite of its invisibility, it is often referred to as "missing matter." Recently, astronomers have been able to detect two kinds of dark (or missing) matter: ordinary and exotic. Ordinary dark matter is the familiar kind of matter. The only reason so much of it remains dark is that it is clumped in bunches too small (less than 0.08 the mass of the sun) to generate nuclear fusion (the burning mechanism of stars) and, therefore, will never radiate light. Exotic matter is dark because it so weakly interacts with radiation, too weakly ever to become luminous. All forms of exotic matter are dark.

Until recently, astronomers met with great difficulty in measuring the abundance of deuterium.[1] They needed to see certain lines in the spectrum of radiation coming to Earth from outer space, and those lines are deep in the ultraviolet range. Since Earth's atmosphere blocks out all radiation in the deep ultraviolet, only a large telescope in outer space would be capable of getting a good look at those lines and at what they could tell us about the amount of deuterium.

First came the Hubble Space Telescope. It gave astronomers a new vantage point. Jeffrey Linsky, University of Colorado astrophysicist, measured those lines and used them to calculate that ordinary matter comprises about one-tenth the "critical mass density" of the universe.[2] (See "Critical Mass of the Universe," page 38.) Linsky's fraction was consistent with early estimates of the total mass of the universe, thought to be close to the critical mass value, and also with the ratio of ordinary to exotic matter (about one to ten). What Linsky did not fully realize, however, was that the region of space where he made his measurements is an area of high nuclear activity, and the level of nuclear activity significantly affects the calculation. Linsky's "one-tenth" now represents an extreme upper limit to the proportion of ordinary matter (relative to critical mass density).

The new Keck 400-inch telescope revealed the nuclear effect and made possible a recalculation. The Keck is so powerful that it can detect the same spectral lines in much more distant gas clouds, where the level of nuclear activity is negligible and measurements, thus, more reliable. A team of four American astronomers observing one extremely distant gas cloud determined that ordinary matter comprises about one-seventieth (1.4%) of the critical mass density of the universe.[3] They are currently observing other distant gas clouds to confirm their result. (*Note:* The latest estimates of the total mass density suggest that it's somewhere between a tenth and a third of the critical mass value.[4])

If ordinary matter comprises 1.4% of the critical mass density of the universe, and luminous stars (ordinary "light" matter) are known to comprise about 1.0% of the critical mass density of the universe,[5] we can estimate that ordinary dark matter comprises about 0.4% of the critical mass density of the universe. Now let's take a look at seven more measurements that help identify "what's the matter" in the universe.

2. MACHOs

For many years astronomers have deduced that the main constituents of ordinary dark matter must be MACHOs (massive compact halo objects), heavenly bodies more massive than the planets in our solar system but not massive enough to "shine," i.e., radiate more than the faintest bit of light. But they had no way to confirm their speculation until the Hubble and Keck telescopes came along. With these new instruments, their speculation has been confirmed. In recent months, two international teams of astronomers have been able to detect MACHOs in the Large Magellanic Cloud, the dwarf galaxy that orbits our own galaxy.[6] The detection was made via the technique known as gravitational lensing (see figure 5.2, page 41).

Other researchers were disappointed, however, to discover that only a few of these MACHOs are faint, low-mass stars known as red dwarfs.[7] This finding means that most MACHOs must be brown dwarfs, bodies smaller than 0.08 solar masses, and thus much harder to detect. Though many more observations are needed to confirm the makeup of ordinary dark matter,[8] these initial results at least prove compatible with the measurements of deuterium abundance and the total mass of luminous stars.

CRITICAL MASS OF THE UNIVERSE

The critical mass of the universe is the minimum density of matter the universe would need to bring about an eventual halt to its expansion. The explosion of the cosmos arising out of the creation event is braked by the gravity of massive objects within it. As Newton explained, massive bodies will tend to attract one another. The more mass in the universe, the greater the braking effect.

---

3. Boron and Beryllium on Elderly Stars

Boron and beryllium are two light (and rare) elements. They are manufactured in the nuclear furnaces of stars. But not in the earliest stars. The first stars that formed in the universe could not produce boron and beryllium because these elements will form only in the presence of ashes from previous generations of stars.

Exotic matter, however, opens another possibility. If there is some exotic matter in the universe, then some boron and beryllium could have been produced in the big bang burst itself, specifically during the first few minutes of it.[9] The amount of boron and beryllium will give some indication of how lumpy (due to exotic matter) the universe was in its early history. This information, in turn, will indicate the ratio of exotic matter to ordinary matter, a ratio that will help us predict even the clumpiness of galaxies today.

Boron and beryllium atoms must be heated up to be seen. If heated sufficiently, they will radiate at high frequencies (that is, they will generate lines in the deep ultraviolet range of the energy spectrum that space telescopes can detect).

HUBBLE'S TROUBLE, COSMOLOGISTS' BLESSING

By now, everyone knows the ironic story of the Hubble Space Telescope. Built at a cost of 1.7 billion dollars and optically figured far better than any previous telescope (to 1/72 wavelength where 1/20 is considered excellent), the manufacturer overlooked a cardinal rule of telescope design—always test the mirrors together, not just separately. The result, NASA's crowning scientific achievement went up in 1990 with a poor focus.

To the dismay of many who were looking forward to crisp, color photos of exotic heavenly bodies, but to the joy of several cosmologists, the schedule of planned observations had to be completely revised. Several of the important discoveries listed here were made as early as they were thanks to the Hubble Telescope's bad focus.

Figure 5.1: Hubble Space Telescope Being Launched from NASA's Space Shuttle

— Photo courtesy of Jet Propulsion Laboratory, NASA.

Fortunately, many of the stars that formed early in the universe's history are still burning, and conditions are hot enough on the surfaces of several of these stars that any existing primordial boron and beryllium would be heated up enough to radiate. Just as with deuterium, though, Earth's atmosphere would prevent us from seeing that radiation.

Once again, the Hubble Space Telescope came to the rescue. Astrophysicists Douglas Duncan, David Lambert, and Michael Lemke made the first-ever detection of boron emissions from ancient stars, one just a hundred light years from Earth.[10] Though this initial result is not precise enough to give us a measure for exotic matter as accurate as that for ordinary matter, it does confirm directly the existence of exotic matter, and it does agree roughly with the amount of exotic matter predicted by the COBE results.

4. Gravitational Lensing

Though exotic matter weakly interacts with radiation, its gravitational influence is the same as for ordinary matter. Because of this fact, a measuring technique refined over the past two years, called gravitational lensing, gives astronomers the capability of measuring the combined total of ordinary and exotic matter. Gravitational lensing is based on the principle that massive objects not only attract matter but can even attract light, literally bending it by the pull of their gravity. Measuring the bend in light coming from distant objects indicates the total amount (or mass) of matter causing the bending. If we had a good measure of the amount of ordinary matter, we could then subtract it from the total matter to get a measure of exotic matter.

As early as 1916 Albert Einstein laid the foundation for this measuring tool. He predicted (using his theory of general relativity) that starlight would be bent by the sun's gravity. That prediction was proved correct in 1919. Since that time astronomers have proved many times over that he was right. The light of stars and radio waves from very distant objects is indeed bent by the sun to exactly the degree Einstein calculated.[11]

It's easy to imagine how much more dramatic the bending is, however, when the lens (the light bender) is a massive galaxy or cluster of galaxies pulling on the light from a distant quasar or galaxy.

The effect is diagramed in figure 5.2 (below).

Observations through ground-based telescopes have led to the discovery of about a dozen massive galaxies and clusters of galaxies, thus far, that serve as gravitational lenses.[12] Measurements of the light-bending power of these objects confirm the presence of a significant quantity of exotic matter, for the pull on the light is significantly greater than the measured amount that ordinary matter could exert.[13] Exactly how much is still uncertain and will remain uncertain until many more gravitational lenses have been found and studied. The Hubble Telescope has the capability of finding one or two per year, and this accumulation will help.[14] In due time we will have a much more accurate measure.

What we can say now, from findings by this technique, is that the universe definitely contains exotic matter, roughly two to ten times as much as ordinary matter.[15] This value is consistent with the COBE

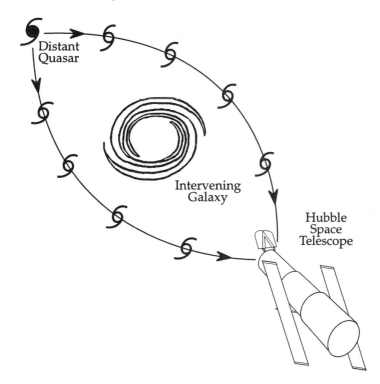

Distant
Quasar

Intervening
Galaxy

Hubble
Space
Telescope

Figure 5.2: Gravitational Effect of the "Lens," the Intervening Galaxies and Galaxy Clusters, on the Light from Distant Quasars and Galaxies

findings and with the measure of boron and beryllium in the oldest parts of the universe.

5. New Expansion-Rate Measurements

An additional Hubble Telescope breakthrough provides yet another tool for determining the total mass of the universe. It's a measurement that fills a crucial gap in a series of calculations.

Let me use an analogy to help illustrate that series and to show where this discovery fits: A friend is driving from Los Angeles to a town in northern California. You know she's taking freeways all the way, and you know that her average speed will be very close to 55 mph. If you knew the distance to that town, you could make a good guess as to how long the drive will take, but all you know is that it's north of San Francisco and south of Eureka. At this point your guess is quite rough, somewhere between eight and fourteen hours. So you find a map that shows the town. With the help of the mileage key you figure that the town is about 550 miles away. Now you can make a much closer guess as to how long the drive will take, and you'll have an idea when to call to confirm your friend's safe arrival.

Finding that distance figure makes a big difference, and that's where the Hubble Telescope comes in. Until recent measurements on a certain type of star, Cepheid variable stars, in a far-off galaxy, astronomers had only a rough figure for the distance to objects beyond the few dozen galaxies nearest to Earth. But since these Cepheids have special qualities that make them reliable indicators of distance, we now have a much better idea of how far it is to galaxies way beyond us.[16] More distance findings are on the way, and they will yield an even more precise measurement.[17] With such measurements in hand, we can use the velocity, time, and distance equations (you may remember from school) to double-check and refine calculations of when the universe began its "trip"—that is, its expansion—and of the velocity at which it's expanding. And we can use these findings to figure out other things, such as the amount of matter in the universe. How? Let's go back to our traveling friend.

If you know your friend began her trip at about 9 a.m., that she's traveling 550 miles, and that a patrol helicopter clocked her on the highway traveling at 55 mph, then you expect her to arrive at about 7 p.m., ten hours after departure. So you call at 7:30 and she's not there. You wait another hour and she's still not there. Now you begin to wonder what's going on. If she is still on the highway, you know she must have slowed down.

So it is with the universe. It has a set of brakes, just as the car does. The brakes in the universe are the massive objects within it. Their gravitational pull on one another slows down the expansion of the universe from its initial explosion. It experiences negative acceleration, that is, deceleration. Since we know the travel time (expansion time) of the universe if there were no massive objects (about 18 billion years), and the travel time if there is enough massive stuff to bring the expansion to a complete stop (about 12 billion years),[18] and since we have measured its expansion time to be somewhere in between these two extremes (15 to 17 billion years[19]), we can calculate approximately how much mass (ordinary plus exotic) is at work in the slowing-down process. We can find out how hard the brakes are being pressed.

These calculations are improving as the numbers involved are being more precisely determined, but so far they tell us that the total mass of the universe is roughly three to eight times greater than the mass of ordinary matter alone, and the total equals about one- to five-tenths the mass necessary to halt the expansion entirely.[20]

The numbers are consistent with the data arising from the measurements of deuterium, boron, and beryllium, from measurements made by gravitational lenses, and from measurement of the background radiation ripples.

6. Detection of Diffuse Hot Intergalactic Gas

The first ever detection of diffuse hot intergalactic gas was announced January 1993 at the 181st meeting of the American Astronomical Society.[21] Three NASA astronomers using the ROSAT (Roentgen Satellite) x-ray discovered a huge gas cloud surrounding a group of three galaxies.

The x-ray emission from this gas cloud was so intense that the three astronomers determined it must be exceptionally hot with an average temperature of ten million degrees Centigrade. The cloud also measured to be very large, 1.3 million light years in diameter. To keep such a hot, energetic gas cloud from disintegrating, the team determined that it must contain between ten and thirty times as much mass as the total visible mass of the three galaxies.

Now astronomers have known for some time that the ratio of invisible to visible ordinary matter in small groups of galaxies is between about three and five to one.[22] That means the remaining mass (ten to thirty minus four to six times the visible mass) must be exotic matter. Therefore, the dominant component of matter in the universe is exotic.

Given this first detection of diffuse hot intergalactic matter, astronomers will be working overtime to discover additional clouds. Once measurements for several more clouds are determined, they should be able to calculate accurate ratios for both the exotic matter relative to ordinary matter and the invisible ordinary matter to visible ordinary matter. At this point, however, the ROSAT results are consistent with the background radiation ripples and the four other methods just discussed for measuring ordinary and exotic matter.

7. Motion of the Large Magellanic Cloud

A breakthrough detection of exotic matter has been made possible by studies of the Large Magellanic Cloud (LMC), a small galaxy companion to our galaxy, orbiting at a distance of about 170,000 light years (measured core to core) from us. (For perspective, consider that our galaxy's visible diameter is about 120,000 light years.)

Three astronomers at the University of California, Santa Cruz, have made the first-ever measurements of the orbital motion of the LMC and have found that it follows an elliptical orbit, completing a revolution every 2.5 billion years.[23] With this information, mathematicians can apply Newton's laws of motion to calculate the total mass of our galaxy. That figure is 600 billion solar masses.

Of that sum, 100 billion solar masses can be accounted for by the luminous matter in our galaxy (stars, gas, and dust). Another 300 billion, at the very most (more likely 100 or 200 billion), can be accounted for by ordinary dark matter (heavenly bodies less than about a tenth of a solar mass each). The remainder must be exotic matter. Determining exactly how much exotic matter and in what form and locations awaits more accurate and extensive measurements of the LMC and other galaxies. But even without such particulars, this additional evidence for exotic matter is consistent with other detections and affirms that theoreticians are on the right track in their increasingly refined model for the origin of the universe.

8. Young Galaxies

One feature distinguishing various big bang models from one another is the timing they predict for the onset of galaxy and galaxy cluster formation. Once research establishes that timing, we'll be closer to an accurate picture of how much exotic matter exists in the universe, for the quantity of exotic matter is a major factor in determining how soon galaxies can form: the more, the sooner, the less the later.

The problem with observing the earliest galaxies, i.e., the most distant ones (due to light travel time), is that they are too faint for the current generation of telescopes to detect. As we look far back, only the strange, unusually bright quasars and radio galaxies are visible. However, a new technique has been developed. This technique is to look for the shadows of newly forming galaxies in the strong light of more distant quasars.[24]

Astronomers Charles Steidel and Don Hamilton of the California Institute of Technology found sixteen possible newborns at vast distances, distances between redshifts 3.0 and 3.5. (The expansion of the universe implies that the spectral lines of galaxies will be shifted toward "redder" or longer wavelengths in proportion to how far away from us the galaxies are.) One of these candidates, an object with redshift 3.4, looks like "a baby galaxy with very little dust," according to astronomers at the Space Telescope Science Institute (the institute that controls the Hubble Space Telescope).

In order for baby galaxies to form as early in the universe's history as the redshift distance of 3.4 suggests, large quantities of exotic matter must exist. Ongoing studies of other very distant infant galaxies and infant galaxy clusters by the just finished Keck telescope and the newly repaired Hubble Space Telescope should reveal how much of and in what different forms this exotic matter exists.

Another Contributor to Clumpiness

As I mentioned in the beginning of this chapter, researchers have found another disrupter—besides exotic matter—of the smoothness of the universe. Specifically, they have observed a distinct lack of galaxies around the most brilliant quasars (distant, intensely energetic and radiant celestial objects that formed early in the history of the universe).

A closer look at these quasars reveals that they are radiant enough to disrupt galaxy formation. The force (light pressure) exerted by the radiation flowing out from such extremely energetic objects is actually strong enough to blow apart giant gas clouds anywhere in their vicinity. And since galaxies begin to develop from such giant gas clouds, that means galaxies cannot have formed within a certain radius of the brightest quasars.

Bright quasars, then, may be responsible for at least some, though certainly not all, of the clumpiness of galaxies. If so, their part in causing the clumpiness may diminish slightly the role of exotic matter. However, it is too soon to tell exactly how much the exotic matter role is diminished. Current measures for exotic and ordinary matter are still too rough, and the maps showing galaxy clumping are still too limited.

Seven years from now, though, the information should be available. By the year 2002, a digital sky survey conducted by the Astrophysical Research Consortium, representing six American institutions, will have mapped a region of the universe more than a hundred times larger than that covered by today's most extensive map. By then, too, Roentgen Satellite and Hubble Space Telescope measurements plus observations through the newly opened 400-inch Keck Telescope in Hawaii should yield much more accurate numbers for the amounts of ordinary and exotic matter.

The Grand Convergence

Together, the Hubble, Keck, ROSAT, and COBE discoveries have helped solve the mystery of how galaxies and clusters of galaxies form out of a hot big bang creation event. The level of irregularity in the background radiation observed by the COBE satellite fits the rough values and ratio of exotic to ordinary matter derived from the Hubble, Keck, and ROSAT measurements. The observed abundances of deuterium, boron, and beryllium match what we would expect from a universe as massive as the gravitational lenses, MACHOs, diffuse hot intergalactic gas, expansion-rate measurements, young galaxy detections, and motion of the Large Magellanic Cloud reveal. These findings all align with the small temperature fluctuations in the cosmic background radiation, and they are not significantly altered by the newly considered effect of quasars. What we are seeing is what scientists dream of. Everything fits together and fits beautifully.

No wonder physicists and astronomers are elated. Their cosmic machine model is coming together. The parts still need considerable grinding and adjustment to run smoothly, but they know they have all the essential parts to make it run.

Astronomers have moved from confidence that the universe was created in a hot big bang to confidence that it began in a particular kind of hot big bang, namely a hot big bang dominated by exotic matter. (This more specific conclusion still permits several options,[25] though one option, a universe in which all the exotic matter is cold dark matter, has nearly been ruled out.[26]) Whenever scientists can move from a general theory to a particular subset of that theory, their certainty about the general theory receives an enormous boost—so much that they will say it's proven. With dramatic proof of the hot big bang creation event in hand, many astronomers have become willing to declare the implication of that proof: the existence of the Creator-God. But exactly how does the hot big bang imply the existence of God? The next several chapters address that question.

CHAPTER SIX

EINSTEIN'S CHALLENGE

Until Albert Einstein's theory of general relativity came along in the early part of the twentieth century, scientists saw no reason to question the notion that the universe is infinite and everywhere the same. After all, the philosophical and scientific underpinnings of this view had been hammered into place by one of the most influential thinkers of all time, Immanuel Kant (1724–1804).

An Infinite Perspective

Kant reasoned that an Infinite Being could be reflected in nothing less than an infinite universe.[1] How the universe came to be is immaterial and therefore unknowable, according to Kant. He concerned himself with how the universe works. His studies convinced him that everything in the universe could be accounted for by the laws of mechanics described by Sir Isaac Newton (1642–1726). On that assumption, he built the first in a series of mechanistic models for the universe.

Kant extended his reasoning beyond physical science into the realm of biology. He saw that a static (life-favorable conditions persisting indefinitely), infinitely old, and infinitely large universe would allow the possibility of an infinite number of random chances. With an infinite number of building blocks (atoms and molecules) and an infinite number of chances to assemble them in random ways (appropriate physical and chemical conditions existing for infinite time), any kind of final product would be possible—even something as highly complex as a German philosopher.[2] His attempt to construct a model for life's origin was abandoned only when he realized that a scientific understanding of the internal workings of organisms was missing.

Perhaps the major credit for Darwinism and the multitude of *isms* that sprang from it belongs to Immanuel Kant.[3]

THE PARADOX OF THE DARK NIGHT SKY

Why does it get dark when the sun sets? This question is not so trite as it sounds. In the context of an approximately static, infinitely old, and infinitely large universe, the light from all the stars would add up to an infinite brightness.

The brightness of a light source is diminished by four for every doubling of its distance. For example, a light bulb at the center of a one-foot diameter globe will illuminate the globe's surface four times brighter than the same bulb at the center of a two-foot diameter globe. This is because the two-foot diameter globe has a surface area four times larger than the one-foot diameter globe. So, since Jupiter, for example, is five times more distant from the sun than Earth, the sunlight it receives is twenty-five times dimmer.

Consequently, if stars are evenly spaced from one another, the light received from them on Earth doubles for each doubling of the diameter of space. This is because with each doubling of the distance from Earth, the volume of space, and thus the number of stars within that volume increases by eight times, while the light received from the stars, on average twice as distant, decreases by only four times. Hence, if the distance from Earth is doubled indefinitely, to an infinite distance, the accumulated light from all the stars must reach infinite brightness. So the night sky should be infinitely luminous.

This conclusion, nevertheless, did not stop proponents of an infinite universe. They claimed clouds of dust between the stars would absorb starlight sufficiently to allow the night sky to be dark even in an infinite universe. They overlooked (until 1960), however, a basic principle of thermodynamics that states, given sufficient time, a body will radiate away as much energy as it receives. Therefore, the universe in some respect must be finite. (See also discussion in chapter 7, page 54.)

As Far as the Eye Can See

As evidence that what we think about the cosmos matters, no century prior to the nineteenth had seen such dramatic change in people's concepts about life and reality. The view of an infinite cosmos in which these changes were rooted received greater and greater theoretical and observational support. As stronger optics carried astronomers deeper into the heavens, all they could see was more of the same kinds of stars and nebulae (gas clouds) they had already seen up close.

Thousands of stars and a few dozen nebulae became billions of stars and millions of nebulae. It seemed endless. Astronomers and laypeople alike were boggled by the immensity of it all.

Further support for Kant's model of the universe came from the amazing triumph of Newton's laws of motion. As astronomers documented the motions of planets, of satellites orbiting the planets, of comets and asteroids, of binary stars, and of stars in star clusters, everything matched what those laws predicted. Kant's claim that everything about and in the universe could be accounted for by the laws of mechanics was substantially bolstered.

The combination of the astronomers' observations and an apparent answer to the paradox of the dark night sky (see box on page 50) resulted in the elevation of Kant's cosmological model from an hypothesis to a theory. By the end of the nineteenth century it was cast in concrete.

Einstein Discovers Relativity

The concrete began to crack, however, almost before it dried. As physicists made their first accurate measurements of the velocity of light, they were taken by surprise (see figure 6.1, below). A revolution was beginning. Here is what would be deduced: (1) No absolute reference system exists from which motions in space can be measured; and (2) the velocity of light with respect to all observers never varies. The velocities of the observers are irrelevant.

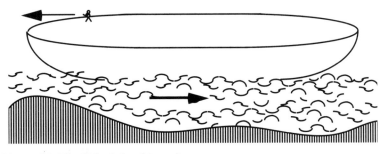

Figure 6.1: The Principle of Invariance
If a ship's captain were jogging around his vessel at 10 mph while the current flowed at 10 mph, the captain would be moving at 20 mph (relative to the ground) when jogging in the direction of the current, and 0 mph when jogging in the opposite direction. This law we have known since the days of Galileo. However, in velocity of light experiments, the motion of the observer proves entirely irrelevant. The velocity of light does not vary with the motion of the observer.

In 1905 a German-born Swiss engineer named Albert Einstein (1879–1955), who studied physics in his spare time, published several papers of enormous significance. Two of them spelled out these conclusions about the constancy of the velocity of light.[4] He called the findings the principle of invariance, but others referred to them as relativity, and that name stuck.

Once this initial theory of relativity (later dubbed "special" since it focused only on velocity) was solidly established,[5] Einstein went to work on the extension of the theory, an effort that demanded every ounce of his genius. The results, published in 1915 and 1916,[6] were the equations of general relativity, equations that carry profound implications about the nature and origin of the universe.

Einstein Discovers the Beginner

For one, these equations show that the universe is simultaneously expanding and decelerating. What phenomenon behaves this way? There is one: an explosion.

When a grenade, for example, is detonated, the pieces of the grenade expand outward from the pin assembly. As they do, they collide with material (air molecules, buildings, furniture, etc.) that slows them down (deceleration). If the universe is the aftermath of an explosion, then there must have been a beginning to the explosion— a moment at which the pin was pulled. By the simple law of cause and effect, it must have had a Beginner—someone to pull the pin.

Einstein's own world view initially kept him from adopting such a conclusion. Rather, he hypothesized in 1917 a new force of physics that would perfectly cancel out the deceleration and expansion factors (see box "Einstein's Repulsive Force," page 54). This perfect cancellation would permit the universe to remain in a static state for infinite time.

Einstein's attempted patch job did not hold up, however. Astronomer Edwin Hubble (1889–1953) in 1929 proved from his measurements on forty different galaxies that the galaxies indeed are expanding away from one another. Moreover, he demonstrated that expansion was in the same manner predicted by Einstein's original formulation of general relativity[7] (see figure 6.2, page 53). In the face of this proof, Einstein grudgingly abandoned his hypothesized force and acknowledged "the necessity for a beginning"[8] and "the presence of a superior reasoning power."[9]

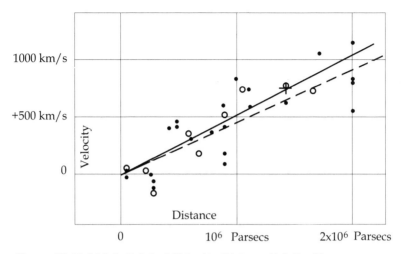

Figure 6.2: Hubble's Original Velocity-Distance Relation[10]
The velocities (kilometers per second) at which several galaxies are moving away from us are ploted against estimated distances. One parsec equals 3.26 light years, where one light year equals 5.9 trillion miles. The cross represents the mean of measurements made on twenty-two other galaxies. All measurements shown here were made before 1929.

As Hubble's plot demonstrates, the more distant the galaxy, the faster it moves away from us. Such a relationship between velocity and distance implies that the entire universe must be experiencing a general expansion.

— *From the Proceedings of the National Academy of Sciences.*

Einstein's God

Einstein's "superior reasoning power," however, was not the God of the Bible. Though he confessed to the rabbis and priests who came to congratulate him on his discovery of God that he was convinced God brought the universe into existence and was intelligent and creative, he denied that God was personal.

Of course, those clergy had a stock response to Einstein's denial: How can a Being who is intelligent and creative not also be personal? Einstein brushed past their objection, a valid one, by raising the paradox of God's omnipotence and man's responsibility for his choices:

If this being is omnipotent, then every occurrence, including every human action, every human thought, and every human feeling and aspiration is also His work; how is it possible to think of holding men responsible for their deeds and thoughts before such an almighty Being? In giving out punishment and rewards He would to a certain extent be passing judgment on Himself. How can this be combined with the goodness and righteousness ascribed to Him?[11]

EINSTEIN'S REPULSIVE FORCE

Einstein's equations of general relativity predicted an exploding universe and, hence, the need for a beginning. To avoid the conclusion of a beginning (and thus a Beginner), Einstein suggested there might exist an undiscovered force of physics operating everywhere in the universe.

Gravity tells us that two massive bodies will attract one another. It also tells us the strength of this attraction will increase the closer the two bodies approach one another.

Einstein's suggested force would work in exactly the opposite manner. Massive bodies would repel one another. And the strength of this repulsion must increase the farther apart two bodies are from one another. Everywhere in the universe, Einstein's proposed force would perfectly cancel out the effects of gravity and thereby allow the universe to remain dynamically static.

This repulsive force was a convenient loophole for another reason. Though no astronomer had ever detected such an effect, Einstein could claim that the reason was the limited distance of our probing out into the cosmos. Today that excuse is gone. Astronomers are seeing and making measurements out to the far reaches of the cosmos. They find not a shred of evidence for Einstein's force.

But, the very idea of two bodies at opposite sides of the universe strongly interacting with one another and not at all when they are up close makes for some very strange physics. As physicist Stephen Hawking put it, Einstein's proposed force was repulsive in both senses of the word.

None of the clergy Einstein encountered ever gave him a satisfactory answer to his objection. Typically, they responded by saying that God has not yet revealed the answer. They encouraged him to endure patiently and blindly trust the All-Knowing One.

Regrettably, Einstein lacked the persistence to pursue an answer further. He took for granted the biblical knowledge of these religious professionals and assumed that the Bible failed to adequately address this crucially important issue. Of what value, then, could such a "revelation" be?

Lacking a solution to the paradox of God's predestination and human beings' free choice, Einstein, like many other powerful intellects through the centuries, ruled out the existence of a personal God. Nevertheless, and to his credit, Einstein held unswervingly, against enormous peer pressure, to belief in a Creator.

I am grieved that no one ever offered Einstein the clear, biblical resolution to the paradox he posed.[12] I am also sad that Einstein did not live long enough to see the accumulation of scientific evidence for a personal, caring Creator (see chapters 14 and 15). These might have sparked in him a willingness to reconsider his conclusion.

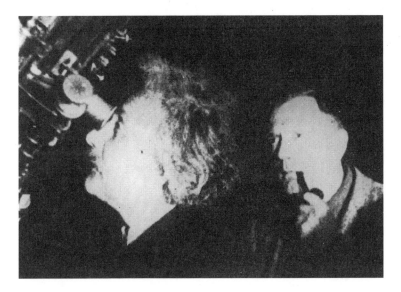

Figure 6.3: Einstein and Hubble
Photo shows (from left) Albert Einstein and Edwin Hubble at the Mount Wilson 100-inch telescope near Pasadena, California, where Hubble made his observations that demonstrated the galaxies are expanding away from one another.

– Photo courtesy of The Huntington Library.

CHAPTER SEVEN

CLOSING LOOPHOLES: ROUND ONE

Einstein fought the idea of a beginning, but other researchers fought harder. Why? Consider how much was at stake, how many ideas, theories, and isms had already been built on the foundation of an infinitely old universe. If that foundation was removed and replaced by one with completely different specifications, much or most of what had been built on top of it would come tumbling down or at least require major reconstruction.

Foundational changes of major proportion have occurred in history, but only through time and struggle. The revolution launched by Copernicus (1473–1543), shifting people's concept of reality from an Earth-centered to a sun-centered astronomical system, took well over a century. Some still resist it today. Ironically, the resistance to both Copernicus's and Einstein's work was fueled by fear of what their new view said about God and the Bible. Sixteenth-century scholars feared a loss of respect for both. Twentieth-century scholars feared an increase of respect.

The desire to keep God out of the picture was no hidden agenda but a clearly expressed one. British cosmologist Sir Arthur Eddington (1882–1944) expressed his feelings clearly: "Philosophically, the notion of a beginning of the present order of Nature is repugnant. . . . I should like to find a genuine loophole."[1] "We [must] allow evolution an infinite time to get started."[2]

The battle was on to protect certain belief systems, especially evolutionism (the belief that inorganic material evolves into simple cells and later into advanced life without any input from a divine Being), and to defeat the notion of a beginning, with its obvious implications.

The Hubble Time

Edwin Hubble's research not only confirmed that the universe is expanding but also measured the rate of its expansion. With that measurement (adjusted a little for the slowing down caused by gravity) and a rough estimate of the distance to the farthest-out galaxies, it was no complicated matter to produce a ball-park figure for when the universe began—the Hubble time. It was somewhere in the range of a few billion to several billion years.

HUBBLE TIME AND YOUNG-UNIVERSE CREATIONISM

Ironically, one of the attempted end runs around the Hubble time has been made by a vocal segment of the Christian community. Rather than seeing the Hubble time as a proof for a recent creation event and thus a strike against materialist philosophies, they see it as proof for an ancient cosmos with time enough for strictly natural evolutionary processes to work. Like many people of the nineteenth century, they seem so boggled by the billions of years that they liken such a time frame to infinite time.

This group of creationists insists that a literal reading of the Bible demands a creation date for the cosmos of only some six to ten thousand years ago. They interpret the creation days of Genesis 1 as six consecutive twenty-four-hour periods.

Not all Bible-believing Christians accept this interpretation, however. As many Hebrew scholars point out, a literal reading of Genesis can just as well support six geologic epochs for the creation days. Both a literal and consistent reading of the Bible, an interpretation that integrates all relevant Bible passages, lends ample support for the creation days being long time periods. From this view astronomy and the Bible are not in conflict over the creation date; they agree.

Readers interested in more detail about this creation-date controversy from both a biblical and scientific perspective will find it in chapter 13 of *The Fingerprint of God*.[3] For a more thorough treatment, see *Creation and Time*, released in 1994.[4]

Whatever illusions certain paleontologists and origin-of-life theorists may have embraced, astronomers recognized that billions of years was hopelessly too brief for atoms to assemble into living things free of any input from a divine Designer (see chapter 16).[5] Therefore, many of them invested enormous energy and creativity in attempts to escape the limits imposed by the Hubble time. Two of these models became especially popular.

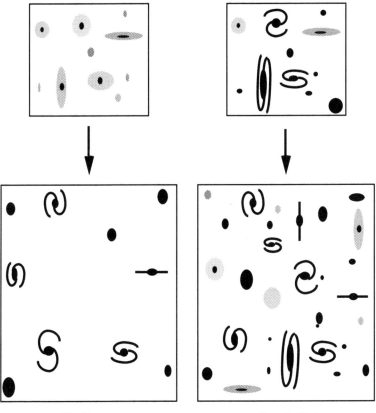

Big Bang   Steady State

Figure 7.1: Big Bang Growth Versus Steady State Growth
In a big bang universe the density of matter thins out and the mean age
for the galaxies advances. All big bang models predict a finite age for the
universe. In a steady state universe new matter is spontaneously and con-
tinuously created. The density of matter remains the same, and the mean
age for the galaxies is constant. On a large scale, nothing changes with
time. All steady state models assume that the universe is infinite in age
and extent. Since the light of very distant galaxies takes considerable time
to reach us, astronomers can look back into the past to see which growth
pattern the universe follows.

Steady State Universe

In 1948 three British astrophysicists, Herman Bondi, Thomas Gold,
and Fred Hoyle, circumvented the beginning via "continual creation."[6] Their models suggested that creation of matter is an act of
nature, even a law of nature, not a one-time miracle from outside

nature. Skipping past any attempt to explain the expansion of the universe, they proposed that the voids resulting from expansion are filled by the continual, spontaneous self-creation of new matter (see figure 7.1, page 59).

The champions of this steady state hypothesis made their theological position clear from the start. Bondi and Hoyle declared their opposition to the notion that anything could transcend the realm of nature.[7] Hoyle made no bones about his opposition to Christianity. To his thinking, "the Universe is everything" and to suggest otherwise is "crackpot."[8]

Failing the Test

During the last three decades a series of complex observational and theoretical tests was developed to prove or disprove the steady state model.[9] Amazingly, the simplest test, devised by Sir James Jeans in the 1920s, was applied last of all. Jeans pointed out that a universe that has no beginning and no end should manifest a "steady" population. That is, the number of stars and galaxies in various stages of development should be proportional to the time required to pass through these stages. There should be balanced numbers of newly formed, young, middle-aged, elderly, and extinct stars and galaxies.[10]

What do we find? A host of "youthful" stars, with ages ranging from a few days to about sixteen billion years. If sixteen billion years seems old, let me assure you, it is not, compared to most stars' life expectancy. The majority of stars in the universe are capable of burning for more than eighty billion years.[11]

In the population of galaxies, the steady state model met with yet more trouble. All, or nearly all, are approximately the same age. We see few if any newly formed galaxies. One was recently reported, but most astronomers agree that it is the aftermath of a collision between two other galaxies. Galaxies in the universe are so tightly packed that such collisions are expected to occur from time to time.

As for older galaxies, we see none at all. Neither are there any extinct varieties. The death knell rang for steady state models when American astronomer Donald Hamilton determined that all the galaxies were formed at approximately the same time,[12] as the big bang predicts.

Under the weight of these and at least nine other independent refutations,[13] plus new evidence that the darkness of intergalactic space must result from the finite ages of all the galaxies[14] (see the box

"The Paradox of the Dark Night Sky," page 50), the steady state models eventually staggered and fell.

EVOLUTION AS EVIDENCE FOR CREATION

Outside of the context of the physical sciences, and especially in the biological sciences, evolution is seen as the adversary of creation. In the clash between the steady state and big bang models, however, we witness the apparent irony that new evidences for the evolution of the universe actually establish that the universe was created in the relatively recent past.

In the physical sciences evolution typically is defined as change taking place with respect to time. Such a definition is theologically neutral. No claim is made as to whether the observed changes are naturally driven or supernaturally driven. In this respect the Bible is "evolutionary" in its teachings on creation since it frames the creation account into a chronology of change through time--eleven major creation events sequenced over six creation days.

The theological thrust of the steady state models was that no personal involvement from God was necessary to explain our existence. Steady state says the universe has not evolved and that it has existed for infinite time. Thus, the dice of chance could have been thrown an infinite number of times under favorable natural conditions to explain the assembling of atoms into organisms.

But, observational proofs now affirm that the universe has evolved, very significantly, from a beginning just a few billion years ago.[15] Thus, our existence cannot be attributed to the natural realm's lucky throw of the dice (out of an infinite number of throws). Moreover, the big bang determines that the cause of the universe is functionally equivalent to the God of the Bible, a Being beyond the matter, energy, space, and time of the cosmos (see chapters 9 and 10).

Scientists lamented momentarily, and yet hope springs eternal. The prestigious British journal *Nature* published this statement from physicist John Gribbin:

> The biggest problem with the Big Bang theory of the origin of the Universe is philosophical—perhaps even theological—what was there before the bang? This problem alone was sufficient to give a great initial impetus to the Steady State theory; but with that theory now sadly in conflict with the observations, the best way round this initial difficulty is provided by a model in which the universe expands from a

singularity [that is, a beginning], collapses back again, and repeats the cycle indefinitely.[16]

Gribbin signaled the change in a new direction for those committed to finding some way around the Hubble time.

CHAPTER EIGHT

CLOSING LOOPHOLES: ROUND TWO

Research that crushed the steady state universe models simultaneously built up the big bang, with its implications of a beginning and a Beginner. Cosmologists who yet resisted this turn of research resurrected a model for the universe proposed thousands of years ago by Hindu teachers and later by Roman philosophers—the reincarnating or oscillating universe. The appeal of this model is that it seems to allow for the relatively recent beginning (as in the Hubble time) while retaining the possibility of infinite or nearly infinite time.

Bouncing Universe

The familiar law of gravity says that massive bodies tend to attract each other. We also know that the mutual attraction of massive bodies in the universe acts as a brake on the expansion of the universe. As you may recall from the earlier discussion of critical mass, the expansion of the universe could be brought to a halt by gravity if the universe contained enough mass (see box "Critical Mass of the Universe," page 38). But that's not all gravity could do. It could throw the expansion into reverse and shrink the universe back to a tiny volume.

Here's where the oscillating universe model shows imagination. It suggests that rather than crunching back into a "singularity" (an infinitely shrunken space representing the boundary at which space ceases to exist or at which space comes into existence), the imploding universe somehow bounces back and begins a new cycle of expansion. Some unknown bounce mechanism is invoked to make this happen (see figure 8.1, below).

According to Princeton physicist Robert Dicke, an infinite number of these cycles of expansion and contraction of the universe would "relieve us of the necessity of understanding the origin of matter at any finite time in the past."[1] The creation event becomes irrelevant, and our existence could be attributed to one lucky bounce. After all, given an infinite number of cosmic bounces, it is argued that surely one would produce all the conditions necessary to convert particles and atoms into human beings through strictly natural processes.

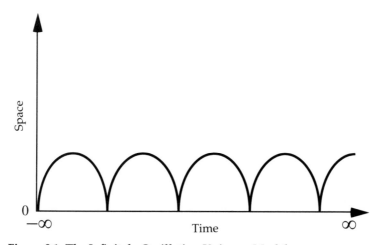

Figure 8.1: The Infinitely Oscillating Universe Model
In the oscillating universe model suggested by physicists like Robert Dicke and John Gribbin, the universe alternates for infinite time between phases of expansion and contraction. Gravity halts the expansion and generates a succeeding phase of contraction. An unknown physical mechanism is proposed to somehow bounce the universe from a period of contraction into a period of expansion, and the characteristics of the contraction and expansion phases are presumed not to vary significantly with time.

In 1965, when the oscillating universe model first emerged as a serious theory,[2] many astronomers launched an all-out effort to find sufficient mass to halt and reverse the expansion of the universe. All the evidence, however, both observational and theoretical, pointed (and still points) in the opposite direction.[3] Even with the new consideration of exotic matter, the total mass appears to fall just short of what would be needed to make oscillation work.

The Rebound Problem

But missing mass is not the only difficulty. Even if the universe did contain enough mass to reverse its expansion and even if a bounce mechanism were discovered or devised theoretically, the number of bounces or oscillations would be limited because of entropy (energy degradation).

The second law of thermodynamics tells us that the entropy of the universe increases with time. This entropy increase means a decrease in the energy available to perform mechanical work, such as bouncing. So less and less energy would be available with each bounce to make the bounce happen.

This decrease in energy from bounce to bounce has two ramifications. First, it means that with each bounce, the universe expands farther out before it rebounds. Picture the action of a ball attached by a rubber band to a wooden paddle. When the rubber band is new, its elasticity is greatest, and it yanks the ball back powerfully. But as it gets warmed up and stretched several times, it loses some of its pull on the ball, and the ball goes out farther from the paddle more easily. The effect for the cosmos is diagramed in figure 8.2.

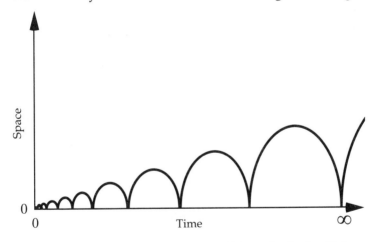

Figure 8.2: Thermodynamic Dissipation Within an Oscillating Universe
Even if the universe conceivably could oscillate, it could not have been oscillating for infinite time. The laws of thermodynamics compel the maximum diameter of the universe to increase from cycle to cycle. Therefore, such a universe could look forward to an infinitely long future but only a finite past. The ultimate moment of creation, at most, could be pushed back only to about a trillion years ago.

Notice that as time goes on the humps grow larger and larger. Looking backward in time, they grow smaller and smaller to a starting point in the not-too-distant past. From the perspective of physics, the universe could not bounce more than about a dozen times—a number far short of infinity.

WILL THE UNIVERSE EVER COLLAPSE?

Discussion of the merits of an oscillating universe model becomes academic if the universe lacks the mass to halt its expansion and force a subsequent collapse. With every passing year, the observational evidence for a universe that continues to expand (the open universe) grows stronger while the evidence for a universe that subsequently collapses (the closed universe) grows weaker, almost to the point of death. The best estimates for the mass density of the universe currently fall between about a tenth and three-tenths of the critical mass.[4]

The second ramification of entropy lies in its effect on the bounce energy. Not only is mechanical energy for contraction lost with each bounce, but so is energy for rebounding. If a rubber ball is dropped from a height of three feet above a hardwood floor, it will rebound, but it will not come up three feet. Some of the energy in the ball was radiated away through friction into heat when the ball made contact with the floor. In fact, each time the ball hits the floor more mechanical energy is converted into heat, and eventually the ball stops bouncing.

A ball with a high mechanical efficiency, for example a volleyball blown up to a high air pressure, may bounce a dozen times before it comes to a stop on the floor. A ball with a low mechanical efficiency, for example a very soft foam-rubber ball, may bounce only twice before it stops.

But the universe has far less mechanical efficiency than a foam-rubber ball. In 1983 and 1984, American astrophysicists Marc Sher, Alan Guth, and Sidney Bludman demonstrated that even if the universe contained enough mass to halt its current expansion, any ultimate collapse would end in a thud, not a bounce.[5] In terms of mechanical energy, the universe more closely resembles a wet lump of clay than a pumped up volleyball (see table 8.1). Sher and Guth confidently entitled their paper "The Impossibility of a Bouncing Universe."

Table 8.1: Mechanical Efficiencies of Some Common Systems
If the universe oscillates, that means it is behaving like an engine or a system designed to perform work. The ability of a system or engine to perform work or to oscillate depends on its mechanical efficiency. The universe literally ranks as the worst engine in all existence. Its mechanical efficiency is so low that oscillation is impossible.

System or Engine	Mechanical Efficiency
diesel engine	40%
gasoline engine	25%
steam engine	12%
human body	1%
universe	0.00000001%

New Speculations

Sher, Guth, and Bludman weren't alone in demonstrating the impossibility of a cosmic bounce. Two Russian physicists, Igor Novikov and Yakob Zel'dovich, developed their own proof based on the geometry of collapsing structures.[6] But none of the five researchers dealt with the theoretical possibilities for oscillation that arise from the quantum gravity era, presumably because so little is yet known about that era (see box "The Quantum Gravity Era," page 68). But it did seem to offer an infinitesimal straw for diehards to grasp.

Arnold Sikkema and Werner Israel grasped it, hypothesizing bizarre effects of merging black holes in that split second when all the matter and energy of the universe would still have been contained in a very tiny volume.[7] These men honestly admitted that no consistent theory of quantum gravity yet exists. It must be noted, too, that the oscillation theory they proposed yields at most only a sharply limited number of bounces. It offers no escape from the notion of a beginning in the not-so-distant past.

That slender straw grasped by Sikkema and Israel was crushed recently by Russian physicist André Linde. At a symposium on the large-scale structure of the universe, Linde demonstrated that the universe, with the characteristics we observe, cannot have arisen from a bounce in the quantum gravity era. Why?

There are two considerations:

1. During the collapse phase toward a hypothetical bounce at least one region or volume (technically called a "domain") in

the universe would utterly resist being crushed to the tiny volume necessary for the exotic effects of quantum gravity to take over.[8]

2. The bounce, if it could take place, would not produce sufficient matter.[9]

Let me explain. The universe, before the hypothetical bounce, begins with a huge amount of space curvature and little or no matter. But, as the universe expands, space is stretched, reducing the curvature. This loss of curvature is transformed into matter, and in the process, a huge amount of entropy is generated. Because of the enormous entropy produced, the process is not reversible. Matter cannot be converted back into the needed space curvature. Thus the universe we live in cannot be the product of oscillation even if the bounces are hypothesized to occur in the quantum gravity era.

THE QUANTUM GRAVITY ERA

Physicists are designing theories to cope with conditions before the universe was even 10^{-43} seconds old (less than a quadrillionth-quadrillionth-trillionth second). At 10^{-43} seconds, the force of gravity within the universe becomes comparable to the strong nuclear force. This force holds protons and neutrons together in the nucleus of the atom. At such a magnitude, gravity may possibly be modified by quantum mechanical effects. Hence this early stage of the universe is called the quantum gravity era.

Since the energy densities that exist during the quantum gravity era lie far beyond the capabilities of even the most powerful particle accelerators, many theoreticians have presumed that they are therefore free to speculate any physical conditions or, for that matter, any physical laws they desire. However, since such physics is obviously beyond "the possibility of observational verification," it would, by definition, fall outside the realm of science and into the realm of metaphysics.

Nevertheless, even though the energies encountered are far beyond current experimental physics, a powerful observational check does exist—the present universe in which we live. If a quantum gravity theory cannot explain how the present universe developed from the initial quantum state, it must be incorrect.

The Reincarnation Connection

Most eastern religions, ancient and modern (including Hinduism, Buddhism, and most New Age philosophies, among others), are rooted in the doctrine of cosmic reincarnation, the oscillating universe. The popularity of these teachings soared in the West with the popularity of the oscillating universe model.

I watched this phenomenon during my graduate student days at the University of Toronto. When several of my peers embraced one or more of the many Hindu or Buddhist sects in vogue, I asked them why. They quoted passages from their scriptures concerning the never-ending cycles of birth, growth, collapse, death, and rebirth of the cosmos and of ourselves as one with it, the "reality" described by the oscillating universe model.

What clinched their commitment, they said, was the amazing accuracy of Hindu scriptures in predicting the period of oscillation, the time between successive rebirths. These writings said 4.32 billion years.[10] Astrophysicists of the day (the 1970s) said twenty to thirty billion years—*if* the oscillating universe model were to prove correct.

My friends reasoned that for the ancient Hindus to get that close to the right answer, Hinduism must be more than a humanly crafted religion. It must come from some superhuman source. This bit of rational support, combined with the enchantment of anything non-Western and nontraditional and an aversion to the moral values of Christianity, was enough to draw them into one of the daughter faiths of Hinduism.

But the rational rug has now been pulled out. Reality is not described by infinite cycles of cosmic reincarnation. The world view underlying Hinduism and its many derivatives has proven false.

CHAPTER NINE

SCIENCE DISCOVERS TIME BEFORE TIME

With the collapse of the oscillating universe model, attempts to get around the Hubble time (no more than about twenty-two billion years since the universe began) turned in a new direction. Holdouts for an infinitely old universe now hypothesize that the fundamental laws of nature as we know them are either incorrect or break down under special conditions.

Escape from Reality
From this new battle front comes the work of amateur plasma physicist Eric Lerner, author of *The Big Bang Never Happened*. Lerner notes that the laws of nature cannot explain the amazing advance in complexity of living organisms that has taken place on Earth over the past four billion years.[1] He acknowledges that this advance stands in violation of the second law of thermodynamics, which says that systems tend to degrade from higher levels of order, complexity, and information to lower levels of order, complexity, and information.

Since Lerner rejects the existence of a Creator, he is forced to conclude that the second law of thermodynamics broke down.[2] And if the second law of thermodynamics broke down for organisms on Earth, it could have broken down for the entire physical cosmos, he suggests.[3] Since the second law ties in with one of the ways we measure time (the rate at which entropy, or energy degradation, increases), Lerner concludes that our observations of the age of the universe are incorrect, that they cannot be used to argue for a beginning of the cosmos just some billions of years ago. There was no big bang, he says, thus no Creator.

The circularity of Lerner's reasoning seems obvious. Starting

71

with the supposition that God does not exist, he reinterprets the laws of nature. Then he uses his rewrite of reality to support the conclusion that God does not exist. Another description of his work is "escape from reality."

Nothing in the physical world can be trusted to exist if we reject the physical laws. We can recreate the physical world into any form we wish simply by imagining a breakdown of the laws of physics at whatever points we deem convenient. But if we do, we have traded in science for science fiction.

No-God of the Gaps

Even working within the laws of physics, researchers with an anti-God bias often make blind leaps of faith to escape any evidence of God's involvement in reality. For centuries Christians were criticized for their "God of the gaps." Sometimes that criticism was deserved. Christians tended to use gaps in understanding or data to build a case for God's miraculous intervention. Then, when scientific discoveries uncovered a natural explanation for the "divine phenomenon," ridicule was heaped not only on those proposing the divine explanation but also on belief in God's existence.

In the twentieth century we see the reverse of the God of the gaps. Non-theists, confronted with problems for which ample research leads to no natural explanations and instead points to the supernatural, utterly reject the possibility of the supernatural and insist on a natural explanation even if it means resorting to absurdity.

For example, steady state models were supported by an imagined force of physics for which there was not one shred of observational or theoretical evidence. The oscillating universe model depended on an imagined bounce mechanism for which there was not one shred of observational or theoretical evidence. Similar appeals to imagined forces and phenomena have been the basis for all the cosmological models proposed to avoid the big bang with its implications about God.[4] The disproof of these models and the ongoing appeal by non-theists to more and more bizarre unknowns and unknowables seem to reflect the growing strength of the case for theism (see chapters 7, 8, and 12).

Time and Its Beginning

Even before the death of the oscillating universe model, a fundamental reason was uncovered for the failure of cosmological models that rejected the finite age of the universe. In a series of papers appearing from 1966 to 1970, three British astrophysicists, Stephen Hawking, George Ellis, and Roger Penrose, extended the solution of the equations of general relativity to include space and time.[5] The result was called the space-time theorem of general relativity.[6] This theorem demonstrated that if general relativity is valid for the universe, then, under very general conditions, space and time must have originated in the same cosmic bang that brought matter and energy into existence.

In Hawking's words, time itself must have a beginning.[7] Proof of the beginning of time may rank as the most theologically significant theorem of all time, assuming validity of the theory of general relativity.

Thumbs Up for General Relativity

What was needed to solidify the proof for the beginning of time was evidence that general relativity really does tell the true story about the dynamics of the universe. Fully aware of the importance of observational confirmation, Einstein proposed three tests at the time of his theory's publication.[8] Within two years, a team led by British astronomer Arthur Eddington met the conditions for the first test when they proved that the sun's gravity bends starlight by just the amount general relativity predicted.[9] This finding generated some excitement, but with a probable error of about 10% in the measurement, scientists were not satisfied.

In the years following, progress in reducing the errors was frustratingly slow. By 1970 five more tests had been added to Einstein's three. Accuracy of confirmation had improved from 10% to 1%,[10] but still not enough to convince all the skeptics. Some theoreticians began to speculate that the universe, though dominated by general relativity, might also be influenced to a tiny degree by an unknown force field.[11] This speculation and imprecision cast just enough doubt on the space-time theorem to dampen enthusiasm for it, initially.

However, as research has continued that small shadow of doubt has shrunk to the vanishing point. By 1976 an echo delay experiment placed on the moon by Apollo astronauts reduced the uncertainty down to 0.5%.[12] In 1979 measurements of the gravitational effects on radio signals further reduced the uncertainty to just 0.1%.[13] In 1980 a hydrogen maser clock (based on the laser principle and nearly a hundred times more accurate than the best atomic clock) aboard a NASA rocket confirmed general relativity to the fifth place of the decimal.[14] When NASA repeats this experiment in 1995, scientists expect to improve the case still further. But all these tests have been made in the context of the sun's and the earth's gravity. What if the context were different?

Strong Field Tests

Compared to the gravity of black holes, pulsars (rapidly rotating neutron stars), and the universe in its earliest moments, the gravity of the sun and the earth are weak (more than a hundred thousand times weaker). Astrophysicists have wondered for some time if departures from general relativity might be observed for very strong gravitational field events.

Figure 9.1: Binary Pulsar
The large, ordinary star on the left orbits the more massive pulsar on the right. The pulsar is what remains from the supernova explosion of a very large star. During the supernova event, it undergoes a collapse so intense that its protons and electrons are fused into neutrons. A single teaspoonful of its matter would weigh five billion tons. The scale here is underestimated. The partner star typically measures about a million miles in diameter whereas the pulsar typically is only six miles in diameter.

The first such tests were conducted in 1982 on the binary pulsar PSR 1913+16.[15] Most binary pulsars are systems in which an ordinary star orbits a pulsar (see figure 9.1). PSR 1913+16 is unusual in that the star orbiting the pulsar is also a neutron star. (Not all neutron stars emit powerful pulses.) A pulsar's gravitational pull on an ordinary star orbiting about it is very intense. The gravitational interaction between two neutron stars orbiting about one another is more intense yet. Initial experiments showed no departures from the predictions of general relativity. But again the error margin was about 10%.

In January 1992, an international team of astronomers published the results of ten years' high-quality observations not only on this pulsar but also on two others.[16] The team applied three separate tests of general relativity to each of the pulsars. In each case general relativity passed with flying colors. In the case of PSR 1913+16, the observed results agreed with the values predicted by general relativity to an accuracy of better than 0.5%.

The 0.5% accuracy figure for general relativity is based on one set of experimental constraints only. General relativity predicts that, over time, two neutron stars orbiting about one another will radiate so much gravitational energy that they will spiral inward toward one another causing their orbital periods to speed up. Careful measurements of the orbital periods for PSR 1913+16 year by year provide an ever more stringent test of the theory of general relativity. With measurements now extending over twenty years (1974 to 1994), general relativity is confirmed overall to an error of no more than one part in a hundred trillion. In the words of Roger Penrose, "This makes Einstein's general relativity, in this particular sense, the most accurately tested theory known to science!"[17]

THE INFLATIONARY BIG BANG

A new version of the big bang model, a model called the inflationary universe, answers most of the previously unanswered questions of big bang cosmology. In the standard big bang model, the universe expands smoothly and adiabatically (temperature dropping due to expansion alone without loss of heat from the system) from the beginning onward. In the inflationary model there is a very brief departure from adiabatic expansion. A much faster, quazi-exponential expansion occurs between about 10^{-35} and about 10^{-33} seconds after the beginning.

There is now little doubt among astronomers that some kind of inflation must operate at some point. The discussion currently centers on what kind of inflation model is correct. A recent development of great theological significance is a paper just produced by Alexander Vilenkin establishing that inflationary models with no beginning are impossible.[18]

So What?

This combination of tests with their successive shrinking of errors has laid to rest any nagging doubts about Einstein's equations of general relativity. Since general relativity does accurately describe the dynamics of the universe, the space-time theorem presented by Hawking, Penrose, and Ellis can be trusted (see the box "The Inflationary Big Bang" for a new development).

This space-time theorem tells us that the dimensions of length, width, height, and time have existed only for as long as the universe has been expanding, less than about twenty billion years. Time really does have a beginning.

By definition, time is that dimension in which cause-and-effect phenomena take place.[19] No time, no cause and effect. If time's beginning is concurrent with the beginning of the universe, as the space-time theorem says, then the cause of the universe must be some entity operating in a time dimension completely independent of and preexistent to the time dimension of the cosmos. This conclusion is powerfully important to our understanding of who God is and who or what God isn't. It tells us that the Creator is transcendent, operating beyond the dimensional limits of the universe. It tells us that God is not the universe itself, nor is God contained within the universe. Pantheism and atheism do not square with the facts.

Pantheism claims there is no existence beyond the universe, that the universe is all there is, and that the universe always has existed. Atheism claims that the universe was not created and no entity exists independent of the matter, energy, and space-time dimensions of the universe. But all the data accumulated in the twentieth century tells us that a transcendent Creator *must* exist. For all the matter, energy, length, width, height, and even time, each suddenly and simultaneously came into being from some source beyond itself.

It is valid to refer to such a source, entity, or being as the Creator, for creating is defined as causing something—in this case everything in the universe—to come into existence. Matter, energy, space, and time are the effects He caused. Likewise, it is valid to refer to the Creator as transcendent, for the act of causing these effects must take place outside or independent of them.

Not only does science lead us to these conclusions, but so also does the Bible, and it is the only holy book to do so.

CHAPTER TEN

A GOD OUTSIDE OF TIME, BUT KNOWABLE

W hen the atheist astronomer Geoffrey Burbidge complained that his peers were rushing off to join the First Church of Christ of the Big Bang, he was on the right track. The space-time theorem of general relativity leads not just to a theistic conclusion but specifically to the God of the Bible.

Of all the holy books of the religions of the world, only the Bible unambiguously states that time is finite, that time has a beginning, that God created time, that God is capable of cause and effect operations before the time dimension of the universe existed, and that God did cause many effects before the time component of our universe existed. Some of the Bible verses making such statements are given in table 10.1 (page 78).

Other holy books besides the Bible allude to extra dimensions, trans-dimensional phenomena, and transcendence, but these allusions are inconsistent. The god and the doctrines these books proclaim always are shaped and limited in some way by the four dimensions of space and time.

The Bible alone describes God as a personal Creator who can act entirely independent of the cosmos and its four space-time dimensions. The God of the Bible is not subject to length, width, height, and time. He is the One who brought them into existence. Moreover, the Bible alone describes attributes of God that defy explanation in the limited context of four dimensions. Some examples are the description of God as a Being who is singular and plural (the Trinity) and the simultaneity of free will and predestination. God's extra-dimensional attributes will be discussed further in chapter 17.

Table 10.1: Some Bible Verses Teaching God's Extra-Dimensional Capacities

In the beginning God created the heavens and the earth. (Genesis 1:1)

By faith we understand that the universe was formed at God's command, so that what is seen was not made out of what was visible. (Hebrews 11:3)

The Hebrew phrase *shamayim erets*, translated "heavens and earth," always refers to the entire physical universe. The Hebrew word for "created," *bara*, means "to make something brand-new or to make something out of nothing." Hebrews 11:3 states that the universe we can detect was made through that which we cannot possibly detect. This means that the universe was made transcendently, that it came from a source independent of matter, energy, length, width, height, and time.

This grace was given us in Christ Jesus before the beginning of time. (2 Timothy 1:9)

The hope of eternal life, which God, who does not lie, promised before the beginning of time. (Titus 1:2)

These verses state that time has a beginning and that God was causing effects before the beginning of time.

"You loved me before the creation of the world." (John 17:24)

He chose us in him before the creation of the world. (Ephesians 1:4)

He was chosen before the creation of the world. (1 Peter 1:20)

The Greek word for "world" in these passages is *kosmos*, which can refer to part of the earth, the whole of planet Earth, or the entire universe. Most scholars agree that the context of these verses implies the latter definition. Thus, God again is seen as causing effects before the creation of the universe, which would include our dimension of time.

Through him all things were made; without him nothing was made that has been made. (John 1:3)

For by him all things were created: things in heaven and on earth, visible and invisible, whether thrones or powers or rulers or authorities; all things were created by him and for him. He is before all things, and in him all things hold together. (Colossians 1:16-17)

These verses declare that Jesus Christ created everything. Nothing was created that He did not create. He existed before anything was created. That is, Christ was not created.

On the evening of that first day of the week, when the disciples were together, with the doors locked for fear of the Jews, Jesus came and stood among them. (John 20:19)
They were startled and frightened, thinking they saw a ghost. He said to them, "Why are you troubled, and why do doubts rise in your minds? Look at my hands

and my feet. It is I myself! Touch me and see; a ghost does not have flesh and bones, as you see I have." When he had said this, he showed them his hands and feet. And while they still did not believe it because of joy and amazement, he asked them, "Do you have anything here to eat?" They gave him a piece of broiled fish, and he took it and ate it in their presence. (Luke 24:37-43)

The disciples understood the impossibility of a physical body passing through physical barriers. That is why they concluded that the form of Jesus in front of them had to be ghostly or spiritual and not physical. But Jesus proved His physical reality by allowing the disciples to touch Him and by eating food in front of them. Though it is impossible for three-dimensional physical objects to pass through three-dimensional physical barriers without one or the other being damaged, Jesus would have no problem doing this in His extra dimensions. Six spatial dimensions would be adequate. He could simultaneously translate the first dimension of His physicality into the fourth dimension, the second into the fifth, and the third into the sixth. Then He could pass through the walls of the room and transfer His three-dimensional body from the fourth, fifth, and sixth dimensions back into the first, second, and third.

Your attitude should be the same as that of Christ Jesus: Who, being in very nature God, did not consider equality with God something to be grasped, but made himself nothing, taking the very nature of a servant, being made in human likeness. And being found in appearance as a man, he humbled himself and became obedient to death—even death on a cross! Therefore God exalted him to the highest place and gave him the name that is above every name, that at the name of Jesus every knee should bow, in heaven and on earth and under the earth, and every tongue confess that Jesus Christ is Lord, to the glory of God the Father. (Philippians 2:5-11)

This passage says that, in coming to Earth, Jesus Christ strippedHimself of the extra-dimensional capacities He shared with God the Father and the Holy Spirit. But these capacities were restored to Him once He had fulfilled His mission of redeeming human beings from their sin.

◆   ◆   ◆

Religions that view the Bible through the limited dimensionality of the universe inevitably deny portions of God's transcendence. Judaism accepts the teaching of the Old Testament but rejects the New Testament. Islam and Mormonism accept both the Old and New Testaments but add other holy books to supersede them. The Jehovah's Witnesses accept the Old and New Testaments but choose to change several hundred words in both. Other cults such as Christian Science, Unity, and Religious Science simply ignore "unpleasant" passages in the Old and New Testaments.

The common denominator in all the alternatives to Christianity is a denial, at least in part, of God's transcendence and extra-dimensional attributes. For example, the tri-unity of God is taught only in the Christian faith.

Suffice it to say, Burbidge's conclusion stands. General relativity and the big bang lead to only one possible conclusion: a Creator matching the description of Jesus Christ. He is our Creator-God.

But Who Created God?

A question children often ask about God is, If God created us, who created God? A sophisticated adult might phrase the question this way: Given that Jesus Christ created the universe and everything in it, including all matter, energy, and the four space-time dimensions, who created Him?

Actually, the question itself yields an elegant proof for creation. The universe and everything in it is confined to a single, finite dimension of time. Time in that dimension proceeds only and always forward. The flow of time can never be reversed. Nor can it be stopped. Because it has a beginning and can move in only one direction, time is really just half a dimension. The proof of creation lies in the mathematical observation that any entity confined to such a half-dimension of time must have a starting point or point of origination. That is, that entity must be created. This necessity for creation applies to the whole universe and ultimately to everything in it.

The necessity for God to be created, however, would apply only if God, too, were confined to half a dimension of time. He is not.

Again, by definition, time is that realm or dimension in which cause-and-effect phenomena take place. According to the space-time theorem of general relativity, such effects as matter, energy, length, width, height, and time were caused independent of the time dimension of the universe. According to the New Testament (2 Timothy 1:9, Titus 1:2), such effects as grace and hope were caused independent of the time dimension of the universe. So both the Bible and general relativity speak of at least one additional time dimension for God.

In two or more dimensions of time, an entity is free from the necessity of being created. If time were two-dimensional, for example, both a time length and a time width would be possible. Time would expand from a line into a plane (see figure 10.1). In a plane of time, an infinite number of lines running in an infinite number of directions would be possible. If God were to so choose, He could move and operate along an infinite time line that never touches or crosses the time line of our universe. As John 1:3, Colossians 1:16-17, and Hebrews 7:3 say, He would have no beginning and no end. He would not be created.

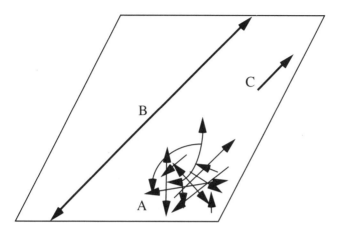

Figure 10.1: God's Time Frame Relative to Our Time Frame
If time were two-dimensional rather than one-dimensional, it would be some kind of plane rather than a line. In this case, an infinite number of time lines (A) would run in an infinite number of directions. This, according to general relativity and the Bible, is the situation with the Creator. If the Creator were to so choose, He could move and operate for infinite time, forward and backward, on a time line (B) that never intersects or touches the time line of our universe (C). As such, He would have no beginning and no end. He would not be created.

Non-Theistic Rebuttals

General relativity and the big bang provide a formidable threat to rational atheism. Recently, committed atheists have recognized the threat and have attempted a response.

The Council for Democratic and Secular Humanism in the winter 1992–1993 issue of their magazine *Free Inquiry* lined up four physicists to write articles under the banner "Does the Big Bang Prove the Existence of God?"[1] The British journal *Nature* enlisted its physics editor, John Maddox, to write an editorial titled "Down with the Big Bang."[2] Atheists have also attempted to revive a plasma model of the universe to replace the big bang.[3]

In the first of the four Free Inquiry articles, Jean-Claude Pecker, a theoretical astrophysicist, questions whether the universe is expanding, and if it is, whether it is expanding at a rate consistent with star and galaxy cluster ages.[4] In the second, plasma physicist Milton Rothman claims, "All of the God theories collapse when three serious questions are asked: Where did God come from, where did God exist before the universe existed, and how did this God learn how to create?"[5] In the third, astrophysicist Victor Stenger looks to a natural spontaneous generation process followed by some "natural processes of self-organization" as the way to avoid the need for God's participation.[6] In the fourth article, philosopher Adolf Grünbaum objects to a theistic explanation for the big bang since it "presupposes some completely fictitious super-time for which no evidence at all has been given." He claims that "it makes no sense to trust [the making of] time as being on a par with [the making of] objects like stars or atoms."[7]

In the *Nature* editorial, John Maddox predicts that since young-Earth creationists have "impaled themselves on the hook of trying to disprove the relatively recent geological record," it will be only a matter of time before "the impatient creationists will have to retreat to the Big Bang" to support their belief in creation. Maddox concedes that creationists' beliefs have "ample justification" in the big bang. For this very reason he declares the big bang "thoroughly unacceptable" because it implies "an ultimate origin of our world" whose cause or Causer lies beyond the universe.[8]

What is Maddox's escape plan? He pins his hopes on a paper by British astrophysicists Donald Lynden-Bell, J. Katz, and J. H. Redmount, which shows that the universe might have begun as a line in space-time rather than as a point.[9]

A Point or a Line?

Let's tackle John Maddox's objections first. The space-time theorem of general relativity does imply that the universe originated from a singularity, but Maddox's definition of that singularity is inaccurate. A singularity is not an infinitely small point, as he suggests, but rather the whole of three-dimensional space shrunken down to a size of zero volume.

Thus it does not matter whether the universe expands from a point or a line. Both a point and a line have zero volume. For that matter, any one-, two-, or three-dimensional shape for the origin of the universe that has zero volume yields a theistic conclusion. In all such cases the universe exhibits a big bang and an ultimate origin for the dimensions of length, width, height, and time. Therefore, Maddox's argument fails. Based on his own words, Maddox's rejection of the big bang flows from his personal commitment to atheism rather than from scientific considerations.

A Numbers Game
Jean-Claude Pecker points to Halton Arp and William Tifft's observations of abnormal redshifts (redshift values that do not match the distance estimates for the objects in question) for some quasars as evidence that the universe may not be expanding. He ignores the fact that the universe's expansion is well established by the distances and velocities of galaxies where no abnormalities are seen. Besides, the peculiar redshifts of Arp and Tifft are well accounted for by the overlap of quasar and galaxy images. Galaxies and quasars so crowd the field of view that inevitably on occasion several will line up in the astronomer's line of sight. What appears to be an anomalous redshift may in fact be another galaxy at a different distance.

Acknowledging that Arp and Tifft's abnormal redshifts may not prove truly anomalous, Pecker nevertheless believes he might still have a loophole. He speculates that the ages of the oldest stars might turn out to be inconsistent with measures of the mass and the expansion rate for the universe.

However, the track record of the observations is just the opposite. As the measuring tools multiply and precision of measurement progresses, the correlation between the measured ages of the oldest stars and the age of the universe becomes tighter. Since the beginning of 1992 we have seen a tremendous improvement in the accuracy of age determinations for the cosmos through measurements of the universe's total mass and expansion rate and through observations of the maximum durations of star burning.[10] These measurements remain in complete agreement.

Other Evaporating Concerns
Milton Rothman stumbles over the question, If God created us, who created God? It's the time-line problem. Scientific and biblical answers exist, but Rothman seems unaware of them. His real barrier may be his refusal to accept any reality beyond the concrete and tangible. He states that the only acceptable theory is one which "permits

questions to be answered in an empirical manner so that we may understand the answers."[11]

Victor Stenger's appeal to spontaneous self-generation at the moment the universe began, followed by billions of years of self-organization that continues right through to the present, is purely speculative. Not one example of significant self-generation or self-organization can be found in the entire realm of nature. In fact, nature shows us just the opposite. Without causation nothing happens and without organization by an intelligent being, systems tend toward lower and lower levels of complexity.

Adolf Grünbaum stumbles over the nature of time. No wonder. Two of the *Free Inquiry* authors correctly quote Saint Augustine as stating that time did not exist before the beginning of the universe.[12] Most Christian theologians to this day speak, like Augustine, of God dwelling in timeless eternity. This leads to the very contradictions that Grünbaum addresses. But the Bible claims (see John 17:4, Ephesians 1:4, Colossians 1:16-17, 2 Timothy 1:9, Titus 1:2, Hebrews 11:3), and science confirms, that God was causing effects before the time dimension for our universe existed. ("Time" by definition is that realm or dimension in which cause-and-effect phenomena occur.) Once this concept of time is understood, Grünbaum's objections to God as the cause for existence of the universe evaporate.

The Biggest Challenger?

What some perceive as a more potent challenge to the big bang comes from Hans Alfvén's plasma theory (plasma refers to high energy charged particles distributed in such a way that they form a neutral gaseous medium). The main point of the plasma model is that gravitational theories alone are inadequate to explain the structure and dynamics of stellar systems, galaxies, galaxy clusters, and even the cosmos itself.

According to Alfvén, electromagnetic effects must play an important role. His point was proven correct for the solar system as far back as the early '60s. At that time it was demonstrated that strictly gravitational treatments could not possibly explain the development of the planets in our solar system. However, the combination of gravity and electromagnetism, as formulated by Alfvén, provided the missing answer.[13]

Along similar lines, Eric Lerner recently has insisted that the big bang could not explain the clumping of galaxies in time scales under a trillion years.[14] He therefore suggested that the big bang model be dumped in favor of a plasma model. But the COBE satellite discovery of temperature fluctuations in the cosmic background radiation, confirmations by balloon-borne and ground-based measurements (see chapter 3), and positive detections of exotic matter (see chapter 5) now establish that Lerner's application is unwarranted. Both galaxies and galaxy clusters can easily form in the relatively brief time scale permitted by the big bang model without any need for plasma at all.

A guiding principle in astronomy research is to develop explanations with the simplest possible theories. All astronomers acknowledge that magnetic fields are present in galaxies and quasars and that these fields play a significant role in the production of non-thermal radiation (the explosive processes at work in the centers of a small class of galaxies called "active galaxies"). However, the magnetic field strengths here are a thousand times less than for the solar system. For larger systems—clusters of galaxies and clusters of clusters of galaxies—the magnetic field strengths are much weaker still.

So far, strictly gravitational theories have been adequate to explain all the observed cosmological phenomena. Nowhere has the need yet arisen to introduce electromagnetic effects.

I believe, however, that the need to consider electromagnetic effects will arise someday. When our observations become sufficiently detailed, electromagnetic refinements to our gravitational theories should provide a closer fit to the real universe. Let me emphasize that what I am predicting is an eventual electromagnetic *refinement* of our best gravitational big bang models. Plasma without some kind of big bang meets with the same failure to predict observable phenomena as does the steady state model.

What is encouraging to theists about these challenges from atheists is how feeble each argument is. The remaining attempts by nontheists to escape theistic implications of general relativity and the Big Bang all fall under the category of quantum gravity speculations. These are dealt with in the next two chapters.

CHAPTER ELEVEN

A BRIEF LOOK AT
A BRIEF HISTORY OF TIME

T hree years ago I was invited to speak to a gathering of movie and TV writers, directors, and producers. My idea was to present scientific evidences for the God of the Bible, but the group implored me to critique Stephen Hawking's book *A Brief History of Time*. A review of a science text for Hollywood media people? It seemed bizarre. But, come the night of the event, the place was packed with twice the number of people expected, and nearly everyone present had read the book.

What I learned that night is that British physicist Stephen Hawking has become a folk hero for many Americans and a cult figure for New Agers. The folk hero status is easy to understand. Who can help but be stirred by the valor of a man who must force the communication of his brilliant mind through the constricting barriers of amyotrophic lateral sclerosis (Lou Gehrig's disease)? His status as a cult figure comes from his reputation for suggesting that theoretical physics renders God impersonal and unnecessary for our existence.

A Brief History of Time is Hawking's fourth book, but his first aimed at a popular audience. It has sold very well—six months on the New York Times best-seller list. More recently it has been made into a feature length film and distributed to theaters around the world.

Most of the book relates the history of the universe to the latest discoveries about the theories of gravity. It is engaging if for no other reason than that one of the key history-makers is telling the story. The chapters on black holes are perhaps the most lucid ever written. Its few technical flaws seem minor. Anyone desiring to learn about research on the application of gravitational theories to the origin and development of the universe will not be disappointed.

Controversial Theology

A Brief History of Time is more than a popular-level text on gravitational theories. What makes Hawking's book unique and controversial are its philosophical and theological pronouncements.

In his final chapter, Hawking declares the goal of his life and work. He bends all his efforts toward answering these fundamental questions: "What is the nature of the universe? What is our place in it and where did it and we come from? Why is it the way it is?"[1] Hawking's dream is to answer these questions through physics alone. Thus far he gives no reason for his refusal to acknowledge, or accept, answers already given elsewhere, specifically in the pages of the Bible. From his close contact with Christians—including his ex-wife, Jane, and physics colleague Don Page—we can assume he is aware, at least, that the Bible addresses these issues. Yet, he chooses to ignore its answers. In an interview for the *Sunday Times Magazine* (London), Jane Hawking said,

> There doesn't seem to be room in the minds of people who are working out these things for other sources of inspiration. You can't actually get an answer out of Stephen regarding philosophy beyond the realms of science. . . . I can never get an answer, I find it very upsetting.[2]

An Absent God

The thrust of Hawking's philosophizing in *A Brief History of Time* is to demean God's role in the affairs of the universe and to elevate the role of the human race. Spearheading this thrust is Carl Sagan, who foreshadows the theme in his introduction to the book. According to Sagan, *A Brief History of Time* speaks "about God, or perhaps about the absence of God." It represents an effort to posit "a universe with no edge in space, no beginning or end in time, and *nothing for a Creator to do*" (emphasis added).[3] Ironically, this message contradicts the conclusions from Hawking's remarkable work on singularity theorems, which in Hawking's own words establishes that "time has a beginning."[4]

Through the principle of cause and effect, this theorem pointed obviously, perhaps too obviously for Hawking, to the existence of some entity beyond the dimensions of the universe who created the universe and its dimensions of space and time. Hawking's only hope, then, for escaping the beginning, hence the Beginner, lay in finding some possible point in the universe's history where the equations of general relativity (on which his space-time theorem was based) might break down.

Even before writing that book, Hawking began to reveal his membership in the ranks of the loophole seekers. In 1983 Stephen Hawking and James Hartle advanced the notion that since we cannot determine conditions in the universe before 10^{-43} seconds (or, 0.0000000000000000000000000000000000000000001) after its origin, perhaps some unknown phenomenon in that speck of time might have disturbed the governance of general relativity.[5] If so, space, time, matter, and energy might not have originated from a true singularity (beginning from an infinitely small volume). They went on to propose that just as the behavior of a hydrogen atom can be described by a quantum mechanical wave function, so might the behavior of the universe. If that is the case, they claimed, the universe could have just popped into existence out of absolutely nothing at what most would call the beginning of time.

This fanciful hypothesis provides the basis for Hawking's widely quoted statement, "The universe would not be created, not be destroyed; it would simply be. What place, then, for a Creator?"[6] It is the basis, too, for New Agers' and atheists' claims that according to science a personal Creator-God need not be the agency for the origin of the universe. To Hawking's credit, he later admitted in *A Brief History of Time* that the whole idea is "just a proposal: it cannot be deduced from some other principle."[7]

Flaw in the Proposal

Even if Hawking's hypothesis were true, there would still be no escaping the need for a Creator-God. As Heinz Pagels, a theoretical physicist, explains:

> This unthinkable void converts itself into the plenum of existence—a necessary consequence of physical laws. Where are these laws written into that void? What "tells" the void that it is pregnant with a possible universe? It would seem that even the void is subject to law, a logic that exists prior to space and time.[8]

Hawking has not gotten around the need for a Creator. Neither has he escaped the singularity. Frank Tipler, another theoretical physicist, has pointed out that Hawking may simply be substituting, unawares, one kind of singularity for another, more specifically a classical singularity of general relativity for a quantum singularity:

> A quantum universe [such as Hawking proposes] . . . necessarily consists of not just one four-dimensional sphere, but rather the infinity of spheres of all possible radii. However, since it is meaningless for the radius of a sphere to be less than or equal to zero, a four-dimensional sphere of zero radius forms a boundary to Hawking's universe. . . . He [Hawking] has eliminated the classical singularity—the beginning of time—only to have it re-appear as the "beginning" to the space of all possible four-spheres.[9]

The God Beyond Boundaries

Hawking himself has argued the case against any real escape for the universe from the singularity and the boundary conditions:

> If the universe really is in such a quantum state, there would be no singularities in the history of the universe in imaginary time. . . . The universe could be finite in imaginary time but without boundaries or singularities. When one goes back to the real time in which we live, however, there will still appear to be singularities. . . . Only if [we] lived in imaginary time would [we] encounter no singularities. . . . In real time, the universe has a beginning and an end at singularities that form a boundary to space-time and at which the laws of science break down.[10]

If we substitute biblical terminology here, we can say that God transcends "real time"[11]—that is, the single time dimension of the physical universe. Thus He is not confined to boundaries and singularities. Both human beings and the physical universe, however, are limited to real time. Hence, they would be confined by boundaries and singularities.

Though Hawking undoubtedly seeks to put some limits on the role of the Creator or, more precisely, to eliminate the *need* of a Creator's involvement in the existence and development of the universe, he is not trying to eliminate Him altogether. He emphatically rejects the label "atheist." He comes closer, perhaps, to fitting the description of a deist. In *A Brief History of Time* he says, "These laws [of physics] may have originally been decreed by God, but it appears that he has since left the universe to evolve according to them and does not now intervene in it."[12] He goes on to conclude that "with the success of scientific theories in describing events, most people have come to believe that God allows the universe to evolve according to a set of laws and does not intervene in the universe to break these laws."[13]

Hawking's reasons for taking a deistic position lie beyond his perception that it is the majority view. He made clear from the outset that he believes there exists a complete set of physical laws that yields "a complete description of the universe we live in,"[14] and further, that these laws "would also presumably determine our actions."[15] Accordingly, "If there were a complete set of laws, that would infringe [on] God's freedom to change his mind and intervene in the world."[16]

Can We Know All?
The most fundamental clash between Hawking's philosophy and biblical Christianity (not to mention physical reality) is Hawking's belief that human beings can discover that "complete set of laws." By this, he means not just a complete and consistent unified field theory (a theory explaining how a single primal force splits into the strong and weak nuclear forces and the electromagnetic and gravitational forces) but "a complete understanding of the events around us, and of our own existence."[17] Elsewhere he has said that he wants to "know the mind of God."[18] Since the existence of the God of the Bible or the existence of singularities would guarantee that his goal could never be reached, it is understandable that he seeks to deny both.

Ironically, his goal is not just biblically impossible but was proven mathematically impossible by Kurt Gödel in 1930. According to Gödel's incompleteness theorem, "no non-trivial set of arithmetical propositions can have its proof of consistency within itself." When applied to the cosmos, this means it is intrinsically impossible to know from the universe that the universe can only be what it is.[19] Normal experience is sufficient to show most of us that our human limitations will never allow us to learn everything about ourselves and the universe. The nature quiz that God posed to Job some four thousand years ago would still stump even so brilliant and educated a man as Stephen Hawking (see Job 38–41). More ironically, Hawking's own words prove his goal impossible. He acknowledges two unavoidable limitations on our quest for more scientific knowledge:

1. The limitation of the Heisenberg uncertainty principle of quantum mechanics (the impossibility for the human observer to measure exactly both the position and the momentum of any quantum entity).
2. The impossibility of exact solutions to all but the very simplest of physical equations.[20]

As Romans 1:19-22 affirms, even a brilliant research scientist can waste his or her efforts, in this case on theoretically impossible lines of research, if he or she rejects clear evidence pointing to God.

All This for Us

Hawking also rejects the anthropic principle, which is the observation that the universe has all the necessary and narrowly defined characteristics to make human life possible. Hawking apparently finds it impossible to believe that "this whole vast construction [the universe] exists simply for our sake."[21] As support for his incredulity, he says that "there does not seem to be any need for all those other galaxies, nor for the universe to be so uniform and similar in every direction on the large scale."[22] But, he ignores a growing body of research. The uniformity, homogeneity, and mass density of the universe all must be precisely as they are for human life to be possible at any time in the universe's history[23] (we'll see this in detail in chapters 14 and 15).

At the close of his book, Hawking suggests that a unified field theory might be "so compelling that it brings about its own [and the universe's] existence." Even if a unified field theory did not create us, Hawking claims, the God of the Bible is not a candidate since we would be stuck with the question of "Who created him?"[24]

Like so many others before and after him, the great historian of time falls into the trap of assuming that God is confined to the same time limitations as we human beings. As explained in chapter 10, Hawking's own theorem answers his objection, an answer that New Testament Scripture had given more than nineteen centuries earlier (see table 10.1, page 78).

Attacks by physicists and other scientists on the God of the Bible are not new. The Bible seems an affront to their intellectual prowess. This ancient "religious" document makes many pointed and challenging statements about cosmic origins, all of them provable.

What an affront to pride. I know I felt it. The call to humility and submission in view of the awesomeness of what God created and wrote is more than some are willing to handle.

No society has seen as much proof for God as ours. But neither has any other society had access to so much learning, research, and technology. These are all things human beings tend to take credit for, especially those who consider themselves the masters of learning, research, and technology. This is what the Apostle Paul meant when he commented that not many who are wise by the world's standards are counted as true believers (1 Corinthians 1:20-26).

CHAPTER TWELVE

A MODERN-DAY GOLIATH

Several years ago an alarm sounded like the one that echoed through Israel's camp in the days of King Saul. The Goliath, this time, was quantum mechanics (a theory defining the energy relationships of particle-sized physical phenomena in terms of discrete levels). Many prominent theologians heralded this giant as "the greatest contemporary threat to Christianity."[1] Besides Stephen Hawking, several famous physicists and many New-Age proponents have proliferated popular books exploiting the difficult and mysterious nature of quantum mechanics to undermine the Christian view of origins.

These attacks seem to express again the defiant reaction to mounting evidence from physics and astronomy that the universe—all matter, energy, space, and time—began in a creation event, and that the universe was strategically designed for life, as the following chapters describe. This evidence is now sufficient to rule out all theological options but one—the Bible's. Obviously, this unexpected turn of research proves discomfiting to those who reject the narrowness of the message of salvation in Jesus Christ.

In their insistence that the inescapable creator-designer cannot be the God of the Bible, researchers grope for a replacement, any replacement. Three quantum possibilities in addition to Stephen Hawking's "universe as a wave function" (discussed in the previous chapter) have been proposed:

1. Quantum Tunneling

British astrophysicist Paul Davies, in his book *God and the New Physics*, written in 1983, locked all cause-and-effect phenomena into the time dimension of the universe. Because the act of creating represents cause and effect, and thus a time-bound activity, the evidence for time's origin, said Davies, argued against God's agency in the creation of the cosmos.[2]

Apparently, Davies is (or was) unaware that the Bible speaks of God's causing effects even before the beginning of the time dimension of our universe. As indicated in table 10.1 (see page 78), the Bible also speaks of the existence of dimensions beyond our time and space, extra dimensions in which God exists and operates.

Davies began by pointing out that virtual particles can pop into existence from nothingness through quantum tunneling (see figure 12.1). Such particles can be produced out of absolutely nothing, providing they are converted back into nothingness before the human observer can possibly detect their appearance. This typically means that the particles so produced must disappear in less than a quintillionth of a second.

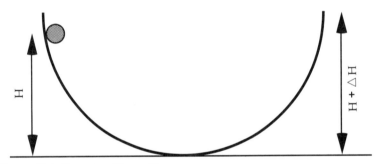

Figure 12.1: Quantum Tunneling
In classical physics a marble released from height H will roll down the side of the bowl and up the other side to the same height H, assuming the absence of friction. Since the lip of the bowl is at a height of H + ΔH, the marble will remain forever trapped inside the bowl. But the uncertainty principle of quantum mechanics states that for a quantum particle there must always exist a minimum uncertainty in the energy of the particle. This uncertainty implies that a quantum particle released from height H has a finite possibility of exceeding height H + ΔH on the other side. The smaller ΔH is relative to H, the greater the possibility. Also, the faster the particle can travel from one side to the other (the less shallow the bowl), the greater the possibility. So quantum tunneling implies that a quantum mechanical particle can escape from the bowl, whereas a typical marble could not.

Davies next appealed to the grand unified theories of particle physics to suggest that by the same means the entire cosmos could have popped into existence. However, he forgot to acknowledge that for a system as massive as the universe, the time for it to disappear back into nothingness must be less than 10^{-103} second (102 zeros between the decimal point and the one), a moment a bit briefer than the age of the universe.

Ironically, Davies' argument against God's creating can be turned against his hypothesis. Quantum mechanics is founded on the concept that quantum events occur according to finite probabilities within finite intervals of time. The larger the time interval, the greater the probability that a specific quantum event will occur. This means that if the time interval is zero, the probability for that quantum event occurring is also zero. Because time began when the universe was created, the time interval is zero, eliminating quantum tunneling as a possible candidate to be the creator of the cosmos.

Of course, some will argue that since we do not know exactly what occurred before the universe was 10^{-43} second old, the possibility necessarily exists that the relationship between time and the probability for certain quantum events in that tiny time interval could break down. However, this argument is based on pure speculation, actually multiple speculations. First one must speculate that a specific breakdown occurred. Then one must speculate that the breakdown occurred at precisely the needed moment of time and location of space. Finally, one must speculate that this breakdown occurred in a such a fashion that the quantum tunneling of the entire universe took place.

WHAT IS NOTHING?

Physicists use the word *nothing* with four different meanings. So it is essential to understand the context of any statement on nothing. The physicist may be referring to (1) lack of matter, (2) lack of matter and energy, (3) lack of matter, energy, and the four-dimensional space-time manifold, or (4) lack of any entity, being, existence, or dimensionality whatever. As our understanding of dimensions beyond length, width, height, and time increases, we can expect other definitions of nothing to be added to this list.

As every student of philosophy knows, anything can be speculated in the realm of human ignorance, including even the nonexistence of the theorist engaged in the speculation. In his book Davies acknowledged the necessity of avoiding such philosophical conundrums by repeatedly appealing to Ockham's razor.[3] Ockham's razor is a guiding principle of Western science that the most plausible explanation is that which contains the simplest ideas and fewest assumptions. The possibility of quantum tunneling as creator of the universe fails to meet the criteria of Ockham's razor.

Davies deserves credit for ongoing reconsiderations and revisions of his position. In a book published in 1984 (*Superforce*), he argued that the laws of physics "seem themselves to be the product of exceedingly ingenious design."[4] In a more recent book (*The Cosmic Blueprint*, 1988) he posed this question: "If new organizational levels just pop into existence for no reason, why do we see such an orderly progression in the universe from featureless origin to rich diversity?"[5] He concluded that we have "powerful evidence that there is 'something going on' behind it all."[6] Davies seems to be moving forward to some form of theism.

2. Infinite Changes

Amazingly, astrophysicists have a reasonably good understanding of the universe's development back to when it was only 10^{-34} second old. We may see some very limited probing back to 10^{-43} second, but that represents the practical limit of research. According to Alan Guth, inventor of the inflationary big bang model, direct measurements of the conditions existing when the universe was less than 10^{-34} second old would require a particle accelerator more than forty trillion miles long, an instrument that in his words had "little chance of funding during a Republican administration" (or in any administration, for that matter).

Another American astrophysicist, Richard Gott, has taken advantage of this infinitesimal period about which we know nothing. He has proposed an infinite loss of information about events before 10^{-43} second. This information loss would occur in an idealized form of Guth's inflationary big bang model, idealized in the sense that the very brief period of the hyper-expansion or inflation of the universe occurs at a maximal rate and for a maximal time.[7] With this total loss of information, he says, anything becomes possible, including "the ability to make an infinite number of universes."[8]

Gott's "possibility" for an infinite number of universes gave some non-theists an opportunity, so they thought, to replace God with chance or, more specifically, with random fluctuations of a primeval radiation field. In other words, they suggested that a random fluctuation out of an infinite number of possible fluctuations in a primeval radiation field could generate a universe with all the conditions necessary for our existence.

This suggestion is a flagrant abuse of probability theory. It assumes the benefits of an infinite sample size without any evidence that the sample size exceeds one.

Consider the following example. If a person spins 10^{1567} (the number one followed by 1,567 zeros) roulette wheels a thousand times each, by random chance, one of these roulette wheels would be likely to produce a thousand consecutive zeros. But if a person had only one roulette wheel to spin, then regardless how many other spinning roulette wheels might conceivably exist, should that single roulette wheel produce a thousand consecutive zeros, one must rationally conclude the wheel had been manufactured to produce nothing but zeros.

Other questions remain. If the universe had zero information before 10^{-43} second, how did it acquire its subsequent high information state without the input of an intelligent, personal Creator? How else but through a personal Creator did a primeval radiation field come into existence?

What we see here is another case of the "no-God of the gaps." It seems that many non-theistic scientists (and others) are relying on gaps, and in this case a very minute one, to provide a way around the theistic implications of scientifically established facts. Surely the burden of proof lies with those who suggest that more than one universe exists or that physical conditions or physical laws were totally different in the period before 10^{-43} second.

Actually, evidence for more than one universe will never be forthcoming. As Gott himself points out, the hypothetical universes in his model remain disjoint.[9] The universes can never overlap. Travel between one universe and another would be prohibited, even in principle.[10]

3. Observer-Created Reality

In popular-level books on quantum mechanics a clear distinction is seldom made between the physics, the philosophy, and the religion of quantum mechanics. Therefore, let me briefly explain the differences:

- ◆ The physics of quantum mechanics tells us there are certain inviolable principles operating on quantum entities. These principles allow the human observer to predict accurately the probability for the outcome of any particular quantum event (for example, an electron moving from one energy level to another).

♦ The *philosophy* of quantum mechanics is the attempt to describe the nature of cause and effect in quantum phenomena and, in particular, the role of human observers in such cause and effect.

♦ The *religion* of quantum mechanics is the attempt to discern who or what is ultimately behind cause and effect in quantum events.

In the '20s and '30s, the physics of quantum mechanics was questioned, most notably by Einstein.[11] But not anymore. The experimental evidence puts the physical principles of quantum mechanics beyond dispute.

A remaining problem, however, lies in the wedding of one philosophical interpretation of quantum mechanics to the physics. Danish physicist Niels Bohr cast such a large shadow over the early history of quantum mechanics research that his "Copenhagen interpretation" has been assumed by many to be one of its basic physics principles. But that isn't the case.

ALTERNATIVE PHILOSOPHIES OF QUANTUM MECHANICS

Of late, the flaws in the philosophical aspects of the Copenhagen interpretation of quantum mechanics have proliferated a variety of alternatives. At last count, ten independent philosophical models have been developed and seriously proposed:[12]

1. A coherent reality exists independent of human thinking.
2. A common fundamental cause lies behind the cause-and-effect phenomena humans observe.
3. All possible outcomes will actually occur.
4. The act of observation dissolves the boundary between the observer and the observed.
5. The world obeys a nonhuman kind of reasoning.
6. The world is composed of objects that possess attributes whether or not the objects are observed.
7. The only observer who counts is the conscious observer.
8. The world is twofold, consisting of potentials and actualities.
9. The real essence of substances is beyond our knowledge.
10. The physical realm is the materialization of pure thought.

Niels Bohr, who operated from Hindu presuppositions, declared that, in the micro-world of quantum phenomena, reality in the absence of an observer does not exist. More to the point, he claimed the act of observing creates the reality. Thus he not only believed a quantum event could not take place without an observer, but that the observer through his or her observations actually brought about the quantum event.

Bohr arrived at his conclusions by noting a difference in a quantum particle before and after its detection by an observer. Before a specific quantum particle is detected, only a probability of where it might be located or of how energetic it is can be known. But after detection, the precise location or energy level is determined. This movement from imprecision to precision led Bohr and his associates at the Bohr Institute for Atomic Studies in Copenhagen to believe that the observer actually gives reality to the quantum particle.

Since the founding of the Copenhagen interpretation of quantum mechanics, others, mainly non-physicists, have applied Bohr's conclusions about a quantum particle to the entire universe. If an observer can give reality to a quantum particle, they say, why not to the whole of the cosmos itself? Of course, these people assume that the observer in question is a human observer. From this assumption, it seems logical to conclude that human beings, not God, created the universe.

Some of the logical flaws in this line of reasoning are obvious; others are more subtle:

◆ There is no movement from imprecision to precision in quantum phenomena. All that happens is that the observer can choose where to put the imprecision. If the observer chooses to measure the position of the quantum particle accurately, he or she loses the potential for any precision in measuring the particle's momentum. Conversely, if the observer chooses to measure the momentum of the quantum particle accurately, the potential for any precision on the position of the particle will be irretrievably lost.
◆ While pure quantum events do exhibit effects that are significant and important, they result in no permanent change to any part of the universe.
◆ The observer does not give reality to the quantum entity. The observer can only choose what aspect of the reality he

wants to discern. Though in quantum entities, indefinite properties become definite to the observer through measurements, the observer cannot determine how and when the indefinite property becomes definite. That is, at some point in the measurement sequence, the pure quantum mechanical description becomes invalid and the physical system assumes a specific physical state. However, exactly where and when this transition occurs cannot be determined by human observers.

◆ Rather than telling us that we human beings are more powerful than we otherwise thought, quantum mechanics tells us that we are weaker. In classical physics, no apparent limit exists on our ability to make accurate measurements. In quantum mechanics, a fundamental and easily determinable limit exists. In classical physics, we can see all aspects of causality. But in quantum mechanics, some aspect of causality always remains hidden from human investigation.

◆ Experiments in particle physics and relativity consistently reveal that nature is described correctly by the condition that the human observer is irrelevant.[13]

◆ The time duration between a quantum event and its observed result is always very brief, briefer by many orders of magnitude than the time period separating the beginning of the universe from the beginning of humans.

◆ For both the universe and human beings time is not reversible. Thus, no amount of human activity can ever affect events that occurred billions of years ago.

◆ There is nothing particularly special about human observers. Inanimate objects, like photoelectric detectors, are just as capable of detecting quantum mechanical events.

All these flaws punctuate what should be obvious to us all—the human race is neither powerful nor wise enough to create a universe. To say that we created our own universe would imply that we can control time and restructure the past.

As time advances, the quantum mechanical alternatives to God become more and more absurd. Today, there are scientists and philosophers and mystics who are willing to claim that we humans are the creator.

The progression toward absurdity underscores these two observations:

1. The persistence of rejection of God's existence and creative work despite the build-up of evidence for both suggests that the source of rejection is not intellectual. This was brought home to me while reading an article in one of the humanist magazines to which I subscribe. The article noted that "atheists, agnostics, humanists, freethinkers—call them what you will—are almost all former Christians."[14] It seems the issue for these atheists, agnostics, humanists, and free-thinkers is not so much the deficiency of evidence for the Christian faith but rather the deficiencies of Christians. They seem to be reacting to their past, holding bitterness over the wrongs or abuses they incurred in their experiences with Christians.

2. The appeal to increasing absurdities in response to the evidences for the God of the Bible demonstrates again how secure these evidences must be. Nothing in our human experience can be proven absolutely. Our limitations in the space-time continuum of the cosmos guarantee this. But when a conclusion is opposed by increasingly absurd alternative explanations, that indicates something about the strength of the conclusion. For example, the Flat-Earth Society still has "reasons" for rejecting the conclusion that planet Earth is spherical. But the reasons presented today are much more absurd than those presented thirty years ago and far more absurd than those presented a hundred years ago. Thus, the history of their appeals for a flat-Earth interpretation reflect the growing certainty about Earth's roughly spherical shape. Likewise, the history of appeals for a non-theistic interpretation for the physical realm reflect the growing certainty about the existence of the God of the Bible.

CHAPTER THIRTEEN

THE DIVINE WATCHMAKER

The evidence for design in the natural realm has always been a favorite argument for God's existence. Though in the past it has been criticized for its lack of rigor and thoroughness, the design argument has consistently proved the most compelling argument for God. That's because the design evidence is simple, concrete, and tangible.

Paley's Watchmaker Argument
A classic historical example of such tangible simplicity comes from the eighteenth-century British theologian-naturalist William Paley and is called "the Watchmaker argument."

> In crossing a heath, suppose I pitched my foot against a stone, and were asked how the *stone* came to be there; I might possibly answer, that, for anything I knew to the contrary, it lain there for ever: nor would it perhaps be very easy to show the absurdity of this answer. But suppose I had found a *watch* upon the ground, and it should be inquired how the watch happened to be in that place; I should hardly think of the answer which I had before given, that for anything I knew, the watch might have always been there. . . . The watch must have had a maker: that there must have existed, at some time, and at some place or other, an artificer or artificers, who formed it for the purpose which we find it actually to answer; who comprehended its construction, and designed its use. . . . Every indication of contrivance, every manifestation of design, which existed in the watch, exists in

105

the works of nature; with the difference, on the side of
nature, of being greater or more, and that in a degree which
exceeds all computation.[1]

No one of sound mind, Paley explains, would ever conclude
that a watch was the product of bits of dust, dirt, and rock being
shuffled together under natural processes. Even if the natural
processes were allowed to operate for a very long time, there would
still be no rational hope for a watch to be assembled. Yet, as all the
naturalists of Paley's day admitted and all the biologists of today
emphatically concur, the complexity and capability of living organisms far transcends anything we see in a watch. If a watch's complexity and capability demand an intelligent and creative maker,
surely, Paley reasoned, the living organisms on our planet demand
a Maker of far greater intelligence and creative ability.

Rebuttals by Hume, Darwin, and Gould

As persuasive as Paley's Watchmaker argument may seem, it has been
largely rejected by secular scholars. The basis for the rejection stems
from three rebuttals: one by philosopher David Hume, one by biologist Charles Darwin, and one by paleontologist Stephen Jay Gould.

Hume argued that the analogy between the watch and a living
organism was not close enough. He claimed that a living organism
only has the *appearance* of an engine, and that, therefore, the complexity and capability of living organisms were only evidences for
apparent design. As to where the apparent design of organisms came
from, Hume hypothesized a universe composed of a finite number
of particles all in perpetual random motion for infinite time. In such
a universe, Hume declared, the random shuffling of matter eventually would produce complex bioforms well adapted to their environment. Such complexity and adaptation would bear to the casual
observer the appearance of design.[2]

Darwin argued that observations within Earth's biosphere established three self-evident truths: (1) tremendous variations existed
among populations of organisms, (2) these variations could be inher-
ited, and (3) all organisms were involved in an intense competition
for survival that would favor the preservation by natural selection of
superior variations. To these three can now be added a fourth: New
variations to replace those extinguished through natural selection are
generated by random changes, or mutations, in the genetic codes

within organisms that are responsible for the inheritable characteristics. Many modern Darwinists therefore conclude that random mutations and natural selection are capable of explaining all of the changes in life forms that have occurred during the history of our planet.

In summarizing the claims of such radical Darwinists, biochemist Jacques Monod says, "Chance *alone* is at the source of every innovation, of all creation in the biosphere. Pure chance, absolutely free but blind, at the very root of the stupendous edifice of evolution."[3]

In his best-selling book *The Blind Watchmaker: Why the Evidence of Evolution Reveals a Universe Without Design*, biologist and self-professed atheist Richard Dawkins declares,

> Natural selection, the blind, unconscious, automatic process which Darwin discovered, and which we now know is the explanation for the existence and apparently purposeful form of all life, has no purpose in mind. It has no mind and no mind's eye. It does not plan for the future. It has no vision, no foresight, no sight at all. If it can be said to play the role of watchmaker in nature, it is the *blind* watchmaker.[4]

This is the heart of the materialists' reply to Paley, the claim that the apparent design and purpose seen in Earth's life forms is not real but rather the product of strictly natural processes.

Gould attempts to buttress the Darwinists' attack on Paley by pointing out a number of "bad designs" in nature.[5] He argues from his examples that living organisms developed by random tinkering, not as the result of any real design. Specifically, he gives the credit to opportunistic utilization of previously existing parts. In his most famous example, he claims that the panda's thumb is a clumsy adaptation of a wrist bone, not the work of a divine designer.

A Reply to Hume

Hume's attack on Paley's watch analogy is unfounded for the following reason: While no mechanical engine is an organism, all organisms are engines. An engine is any system capable of processing energy to perform work. All organisms do this. But they do a lot more. Thus, since no one would rationally argue that a working engine designed by another human could be chance-assembled by purely natural processes, it is far more ludicrous to suggest that strictly natural processes could assemble living organisms.

Hume made his argument before astronomers could measure the cosmos. He did not know his necessary condition for the natural assembly of bioforms, namely infinite time, was false. Neither did he know that suitable conditions for life chemistry have existed for only a brief portion of the universe's duration.

Hume also wrote before biologists were capable of appreciating the incredible complexity and functionality of living organisms. Statistical mechanics tells us that if the means to preserve the initial and intermediate stages of assembly are absent, the greater the complexity and functionality of a system, the less advantageous additional time becomes for assembly by random processes (the parts wear out too soon). Moreover, assembly is not enough. Just as the assembled watch must first be wound up and the time set before it is able to function, so also something or Someone must set the assembled organism into operation.

The Origins Question
A major flaw in the attack by radical Darwinists on the Watchmaker argument is their failure to address the origin of life. The Darwinist mechanisms of natural selection and mutations are useless *until the first life form is assembled*. In spite of decades of intense research, origin-of-life scientists have yet to demonstrate the feasibility of any mechanism(s) for the assembly of a living organism from inorganic materials by strictly natural processes (see chapter 16). Here the analogy with Paley's watch remains quite close. Both have a high degree of complexity, and both move from zero functionality to complete functionality.

Another flaw is that, just like Hume, Darwin failed to understand that the geologic eras do not provide even remotely sufficient time for living organisms to change significantly by natural processes. While it is beyond dispute that life forms have changed very significantly over the course of the history of planet Earth, only micro-evolutionary changes have been determined to occur by strictly natural processes.

Natural selection can move a species only a limited distance from the species' norm, and the greater the distance, the lower the probability for survival. A good example of these limitations is demonstrated in dog breeding. One cannot possibly breed a dog significantly smaller than a teacup poodle. Moreover, such a poodle requires an intense level of care just to survive. More tellingly, if all the dog breeds were allowed to interact sexually, they would quickly revert back to their wild dog ancestries.

For macro-evolution to occur by strictly natural processes, multiple favorable mutations must take place simultaneously at a rate sufficient to overcome the natural extinction rate. This leads to an insurmountable problem.

Evolution Reversal

According to the fossil record, more and more species of life came into existence through the millennia before the appearance of modern humans. Through time, the number of species extinctions nearly balanced the number of introductions, but introductions remained slightly more numerous.

Everything changed, however, with the arrival of the human species. Since the first human being, the number of species going extinct has remained high while the number of new species appearing measures a virtual zero. Estimates of the current rate of extinction vary, from a low of one species per day to a high of five species per hour.[6] Though many believe that the influence of the human race on that rate predominates, environmental experts are willing to say that even if no humans existed, at least one species per year would still go extinct.[7] Meanwhile, as biologists Paul and Anne Ehrlich disclose, "The production of a new animal species in nature has yet to be documented." Furthermore, "in the vast majority of cases, the rate of change is so slow that it has not even been possible to detect an increase in the amount of differentiation."[8] Obviously, a tremendous imbalance between extinctions and speciation now exists.

The imbalance between speciation today and speciation in the fossil record era cannot be explained by radically different natural conditions. The conditions are known, and they are not significantly different. What is different is God's activity. The Bible declares that God has currently ceased from His work of creating new life forms. But in the fossil record era (God's six days of creation), God was active in creating millions of species of life, introducing new species and replacing and upgrading all those going extinct by natural processes.

What the materialists fail to address in their Darwinist musings is the reversal in the direction of biological evolution. Before the appearance of the human race, life on Earth was becoming progressively complex and diverse (during God's days of creation). But after the appearance of human beings, life on Earth is becoming less complex and diverse (since God's seventh day of rest).

Much more could be added to the argument against the materialistic interpretation of life, such as the problems of mass extinctions, similarities in chemistry and form among Earth's species, the origin of sex, non-random mutations, missing horizontal branches in the fossil record tree, genetic decay, etc. But space does not permit. Modern research in astronomy, biology, and paleontology, far from discrediting Paley, fully exonerate him.

A Bad Design?

As for Gould's examples of bad design, three responses come to mind. The first is that his judging of certain biological components as bad is largely subjective. Others have disagreed with his evaluations. In particular, Peter Gordon takes issue with Gould's best-known example of the panda's thumb. Gordon argues that rather than the thumb being clumsy and jury-rigged, it is a functional, original design.[9]

Organisms are so complex that no biologist can claim to understand them completely. Thus, even biologists are in a poor position to judge the quality of the Creator's work.

A second response is that to believe in creation by God is not to claim that all the development in organisms is strictly divine. In addition to divine intervention, natural processes are obviously at work to change, at least to some degree, the form and function of organisms. Thus the second law of thermodynamics, for example, would guarantee increasing degradation of the divine designs.

A third response is that Gould provides no new explanation for the design in the "previously existing parts." All he can muster are the already discredited Darwinist explanations.

A Better Argument

Far from being shattered, Paley's Watchmaker argument stands firm. But an obvious way to strengthen Paley's argument is to look at the whole in addition to the part. Paley did the only thing he could do: examine a tiny part of God's creation in search of evidence for Him. That left unanswered, however, the relationship of the whole to the part. But this is a relationship that can now be explored. The universe now has been measured and new understandings of the whole help us to comprehend more about the Creator.

CHAPTER FOURTEEN

A "JUST RIGHT" UNIVERSE

No other generation has witnessed so many discoveries about the universe. No other generation has seen the measuring of the cosmos. For previous generations the universe remained a profound mystery. But we are alive to see several of its mysteries solved.

Not only can we measure certain aspects of the universe, but in these measurements we are discovering some of the characteristics of the One who fashioned it all. Astronomy has provided us with new tools to probe the Creator's personality.

Building Blocks Problem
Before the measuring of the cosmos, non-theists assumed the availability of the appropriate building blocks for life. They posited that, with enough time, the right natural processes, and enough building blocks, even systems as complex as organisms could be assembled without the help of a supreme being. In chapters 3, 7, 8, and 9, we have seen there is not sufficient time. In this chapter we'll consider just how amazing it is that the universe provides the right building blocks and the right natural processes for life.

To put this situation in perspective, imagine the possibility of a Boeing 747 aircraft being completely assembled as a result of a tornado striking a junkyard. Now imagine how much more unlikely that possibility would be if bauxite (aluminum ore) is substituted for the junk parts. Finally, imagine the possibility if instead of bauxite, river silt is substituted. So, too, as one examines the building blocks necessary for life to come into existence, the possibility of that happening without someone or something designing them stretches the imagination beyond the breaking point. Four major building blocks must be designed "just right" for life.

1. Getting the Right Molecules

For life to be possible, more than forty different elements must be able to bond together to form molecules. Molecular bonding depends on two factors, the strength of the force of electromagnetism and the ratio of the mass of the electron to the mass of the proton.

If the electromagnetic force were significantly larger, atoms would hang on to electrons so tightly no sharing of electrons with other atoms would be possible. But if the electromagnetic force were significantly weaker, atoms would not hang on to electrons at all, and again, the sharing of electrons among atoms, which makes molecules possible, would not take place. If more than just a few kinds of molecules are to exist, the electromagnetic force must be more delicately balanced yet.

The size and stability of electron orbits about the nuclei of atoms depends on the ratio of the electron mass to the proton mass. Unless this ratio is delicately balanced, the chemical bondings essential for life chemistry could never take place.

2. Getting the Right Atoms

Life molecules cannot be built unless sufficient quantities of the elements essential for life are available. This means atoms of various sizes must be able to form. For that to happen, a delicate balance must exist for each of the constants of physics governing the strong and weak nuclear forces, and gravity, also for the nuclear ground state energies (quantum energy levels important for the forming of elements from protons and neutrons) for several key elements.

In the case of the strong nuclear force—the force governing the degree to which protons and neutrons stick together in atomic nuclei—the balance is easy to see. If this force were too weak, protons and neutrons would not stick together. In that case, only one element would exist in the universe, hydrogen, because the hydrogen atom has only one proton and no neutrons in its nucleus. On the other hand, if the strong nuclear force were of slightly greater strength than what we observe in the cosmos, protons and neutrons would have such an affinity for one another that not one would remain alone. They would all find themselves attached to many other protons and neutrons. In such a universe there would be no hydrogen, only heavy elements. Life chemistry is impossible without hydrogen; it is also impossible if hydrogen is the only element.

How delicate is the balance for the strong nuclear force? If it were just 2% weaker or 0.3% stronger than it actually is, life would be impossible at any time and any place within the universe.[1]

Are we just considering life as we know it? No, we're talking about any conceivable kind of life chemistry throughout the cosmos. This delicate condition must be met universally.

In the case of the weak nuclear force—the force that governs, among other things, the rates of radioactive decay—if it were much stronger than what we observe, the matter in the universe would quickly be converted into heavy elements. But if it were much weaker, the matter in the universe would remain in the form of just the lightest elements. Either way, the elements essential for life chemistry (such as carbon, oxygen, nitrogen, phosphorus) either would not exist at all or would exist in amounts far too small for all the life-essential chemicals to be built. Further, unless the weak nuclear force were delicately balanced, those life-essential elements that are produced only in the cores of supergiant stars would never escape the boundaries of those cores (supernova explosions would become impossible).[2]

The strength of the force of gravity determines how hot the nuclear furnaces in the cores of stars will burn. If the gravitational force were any stronger, stars would be so hot they would burn up relatively quickly, too quickly and too erratically for life. Additionally, a planet capable of sustaining life must be supported by a star that is both stable and long burning. However, if the gravitational force were any weaker, stars never would become hot enough to ignite nuclear fusion. In such a universe no elements heavier than hydrogen and helium would be produced.

In the late 1970s and early 1980s, Fred Hoyle discovered that an incredible fine tuning of the nuclear ground state energies for helium, beryllium, carbon, and oxygen was necessary for any kind of life to exist. The ground state energies for these elements cannot be higher or lower with respect to each other by more than 4% without yielding a universe with insufficient oxygen or carbon for life.[3] Hoyle, who has written extensively against theism[4] and Christianity in particular,[5] nevertheless concluded on the basis of this quadruple fine tuning that "a superintellect has monkeyed with physics, as well as with chemistry and biology."[6]

3. Getting the Right Nucleons
One must monkey with the physics of the universe to get enough of the right elements for life, and further to get those elements to join

together to form life molecules. One must also fine tune the universe to get enough nucleons (protons and neutrons) to form the elements.

In the first moments after creation, the universe contained about ten billion and one nucleons for every ten billion anti-nucleons. The ten billion anti-nucleons annihilated the ten billion nucleons, generating an enormous amount of energy. All the galaxies and stars that make up the universe today were formed from the leftover nucleons. If the initial excess of nucleons over anti-nucleons were any smaller, there would not be enough matter for galaxies, stars, and heavy elements to form. If the excess were any greater, galaxies would form, but they would so efficiently condense and trap radiation that none of them would fragment to form stars and planets.

The neutron is 0.138% more massive than a proton. Because of this extra mass, neutrons require slightly more energy to make than protons. So as the universe cooled from the hot big bang creation event, it produced more protons than neutrons—in fact, about seven times as many.

If the neutron were just another 0.1% more massive, so few neutrons would remain from the cooling off of the big bang that there would not be enough of them to make the nuclei of all the heavy elements essential for life. The extra mass of the neutron relative to the proton also determines the rate at which neutrons decay into protons and protons build into neutrons (one neutron = one proton + one electron + one neutrino). If the neutron were 0.1% less massive, so many protons would be built up to make neutrons that all the stars in the universe would have rapidly collapsed into either neutron stars or black holes.[7] Thus for life to be possible in the universe, the neutron mass must be fine tuned to better than 0.1%.

Another decay process involving protons must also be fine-tuned for life to exist. Protons are believed to decay into mesons (a type of fundamental particle). I say "believed to" because the decay rate is so slow experimenters have yet to record a single decay event (average decay time for a single proton exceeds 4×10^{32} years). Nevertheless, theoreticians are convinced that protons must decay into mesons, and at a rate fairly close to the current experimental limits. If protons decay any slower into mesons, the universe of today would not have enough nucleons to make the necessary galaxies, stars, and planets.[8] This is because the factors that determine this decay rate also determine the ratio of nucleons to antinucleons at the time of the creation event. Thus, if the decay rate were slower, the number of nucleons would have been too closely balanced by the number of antinucleons, which after annihilation would have left too few nucleons.

If, however, the decay rate of protons into mesons were faster, in addition to the problem of a too large ratio of nucleons to antinucleons, there would also be an additional problem from the standpoint of maintaining life. Because a tremendous amount of energy is released in this particular decay process, the rate of decay would destroy or harm life. Thus the decay rate cannot be any greater than it is.

4. Getting the Right Electrons

Not only must the universe be fine tuned to get enough nucleons, but also a precise number of electrons must exist. Unless the number of electrons is equivalent to the number of protons to an accuracy of one part in 10^{37}, or better, electromagnetic forces in the universe would have so overcome gravitational forces that galaxies, stars, and planets never would have formed.

One part in 10^{37} is such an incredibly sensitive balance that it is hard to visualize. The following analogy might help: Cover the entire North American continent in dimes all the way up to the moon, a height of about 239,000 miles. (In comparison, the money to pay for the U.S. federal government debt would cover one square mile less than two feet deep with dimes.) Next, pile dimes from here to the moon on a billion other continents the same size as North America. Paint one dime red and mix it into the billion piles of dimes. Blindfold a friend and ask him to pick out one dime. The odds that he will pick the red dime are one in 10^{37}. And this is only one of the parameters that is so delicately balanced to allow life to form.

At whatever level we examine the building blocks of life—electrons, nucleons, atoms, or molecules—the physics of the universe must be very meticulously fine tuned. The universe must be exactingly constructed to create the necessary electrons. It must be exquisitely crafted to produce the protons and neutrons required. It must be carefully fabricated to obtain the needed atoms. Unless it is skillfully fashioned, the atoms will not be able to assemble into complex enough molecules. Such precise balancing of all these factors is truly beyond our ability to comprehend. Yet with the measuring of the universe, even more astounding facts become apparent.

Cosmos' Expansion

The first parameter of the universe to be measured was the universe's expansion rate. In comparing this rate to the physics of galaxy and star formation, astrophysicists found something amazing. If the universe expanded too rapidly, matter would disperse so efficiently that none of it would clump enough to form galaxies. If no galaxies form, no stars will form. If no stars form, no planets will form. If no planets form, there's no place for life. On the other hand, if the universe expanded too slowly, matter would clump so effectively that all of it, the whole universe in fact, would collapse into a super-dense lump before any solar-type stars could form.

What's even more amazing is how delicately balanced that expansion rate must be for life to exist. It cannot differ by more than one part in 10^{55} from the actual rate.

An analogy that still does not come close to describing the precarious nature of this balance would be a million pencils all simultaneously positioned upright on their points on a smooth glass surface with no external supports.

The inflationary big bang model for the universe offers a physical explanation for why the universe is poised so delicately in its expansion rate. As the four fundamental forces of physics (the forces of gravity, strong nuclear, weak nuclear, and electromagnetic) separated from one another during the first split second after the creation event, it is possible to have a brief period of hyperinflation (lasting only 10^{-34} seconds) that virtually guarantees the universe later on will expand at a rate that permits life to exist. Of course, what that does is trade one exquisite balance (the expansion rate of the cosmos) for another (the values of a set of several constants of physics).

In addition to requiring exquisite fine-tuning of the forces and constants of physics, the existence of life demands still more. It demands that the fundamental particles, the energy, and the space-time dimensions of the universe enable the principles of quantum tunneling and special relativity to operate exactly as they do. Quantum tunneling must function no more or less efficiently than what we observe for hemoglobin to transport the right amount of oxygen to the cells of all vertebrate and most invertebrate species.[9] Likewise, relativistic corrections, not too great and not too small, are essential in order for copper and vanadium to fulfill their critical roles in the functioning of the nervous system and bone development of all the higher animals.[10]

Measuring the Universe's Age

The second parameter of the universe to be measured was its age. For many decades astronomers and others have wondered why, given God exists, He would wait so many billions of years to make life. Why did He not do it right away? The answer is that, given the laws and constants of physics God chose to create, it takes about ten to twelve billion years just to fuse enough heavy elements in the nuclear furnaces of several generations of giant stars to make life chemistry possible.

Life could not happen any earlier in the universe than it did on Earth. Nor could it happen much later. As the universe ages, stars like the sun—located in the right part of the galaxy for life (see chapter 15) and in a stable nuclear burning phase—become increasingly rare. If the universe were just a few billion years older, such stars would no longer exist.

A third parameter that I already discussed to some extent is entropy, or energy degradation. In chapter 3, I explained the evidence for the universe possessing an extreme amount of specific entropy. This high level of entropy is essential for life. Without it, systems as small as stars and planets would never form. But as extremely high as the entropy of the universe is, it could not be much higher. If it were higher, systems as large as galaxies would never form. Stars and planets cannot form without galaxies.

Star Masses

A fourth parameter, another very sensitive one, is the ratio of the electromagnetic force constant to the gravitational force constant. If the electromagnetic force relative to gravity were increased by just one part in 10^{40}, only small stars would form. And, if it were decreased by just one part in 10^{40}, only large stars would form. But for life to be possible in the universe, both large and small stars must exist. The large stars must exist because only in their thermonuclear furnaces are most of the life-essential elements produced. The small stars like the sun must exist because only small stars burn long enough and stably enough to sustain a planet with life.[11]

Considering again the piles of dimes, one part in 10^{40} is equivalent to a blindfolded person rummaging through a trillion piles of dimes the size of North America that reach to the moon and picking out, on the first try, the one red dime.

In the late '80s and early '90s, several other characteristics of the universe were measured successfully. Each of these, too, indicated a careful fine tuning for the support of life. Currently, researchers have uncovered twenty-six characteristics that must take on narrowly defined values for life of any kind to possibly exist. A list of these characteristics and the reasons they must be so narrowly defined is given in table 14.1.

The list of finely tuned characteristics for the universe continues to grow. Parameters 24, 25, and 26, for example, were added just in the last several months.[13] The more accurately and extensively astronomers measure the universe, the more finely tuned they discover it to be. Also, as we have seen for many of the already measured characteristics, the degree of fine tuning is utterly amazing—far beyond what human endeavors can accomplish.

For example, arguably the best machine ever built by man is a brand new gravity wave detector engineered by California Institute of Technology physicists to make measurements accurate to one part in 10^{23}. By comparison, three different characteristics of the universe must be fine-tuned to better than one part in 10^{37} for life of any kind to exist (for comment on why life must be carbon-based, see section entitled "Another Kind of Life" on pages 133–134). My point is that the Entity who brought the universe into existence must be a personal Being, for only a person can design with anywhere near this degree of precision. Consider, too, that this personal Entity must be at least a hundred trillion times more "capable" than are we human beings with all our resources.

Table 14.1: Evidence for the Fine Tuning of the Universe[12]
More than two dozen parameters for the universe must have values falling within narrowly defined ranges for life of any kind to exist.

1. strong nuclear force constant
   if larger: no hydrogen; nuclei essential for
      life would be unstable
   if smaller: no elements other than hydrogen
2. weak nuclear force constant
   if larger: too much hydrogen converted to helium in big bang, hence too
      much heavy element material made by star burning; no expulsion
      of heavy elements from stars
   if smaller: too little helium produced from big bang, hence too little
      heavy element material made by star burning; no expulsion of
      heavy elements from stars
3. gravitational force constant
   if larger: stars would be too hot and would burn up too quickly and too
      unevenly

if smaller: stars would remain so cool that nuclear fusion would never ignite, hence no heavy element production

4. electromagnetic force constant

if larger: insufficient chemical bonding; elements more massive than boron would be too unstable for fission

if smaller: insufficient chemical bonding

5. ratio of electromagnetic force constant to gravitational force constant

if larger: no stars less than 1.4 solar masses, hence short stellar life spans and uneven stellar luminosities

if smaller: no stars more than 0.8 solar masses, hence no heavy element production

6. ratio of electron to proton mass

if larger: insufficient chemical bonding

if smaller: insufficient chemical bonding

7. ratio of numbers of protons to electrons

if larger: electromagnetism would dominate gravity, preventing galaxy, star, and planet formation

if smaller: electromagnetism would dominate gravity, preventing galaxy, star, and planet formation

8. expansion rate of the universe

if larger: no galaxy formation

if smaller: universe would collapse prior to star formation

9. entropy level of the universe

if smaller: no proto-galaxy formation

if larger: no star condensation within the proto-galaxies

10. mass density of the universe

if larger: too much deuterium from big bang, hence stars burn too rapidly

if smaller: insufficient helium from big bang, hence too few heavy elements forming

11. velocity of light

if faster: stars would be too luminous

if slower: stars would not be luminous enough

12. age of the universe

if older: no solar-type stars in a stable burning phase in the right part of the galaxy

if younger: solar-type stars in a stable burning phase would not yet have formed

13. initial uniformity of radiation

if smoother: stars, star clusters, and galaxies would not have formed

if coarser: universe by now would be mostly black holes and empty space

14. fine structure constant (a number used to describe the fine

structure splitting of spectral lines)

    if larger: DNA would be unable to function; no stars more
        than 0.7 solar masses

    if smaller: DNA would be unable to function; no stars less than 1.8
        solar masses

15. average distance between galaxies

    if larger: insufficient gas would be infused into our galaxy to
        sustain star formation over an adequate time span

    if smaller: the sun's orbit would be too radically disturbed

16. average distance between stars

    if larger: heavy element density too thin for rocky planets to form

    if smaller: planetary orbits would become destabilized

17. decay rate of the proton

    if greater: life would be exterminated by the release of radiation

    if smaller: insufficient matter in the universe for life

18. ^{12}Carbon (^{12}C) to ^{16}Oxygen (^{16}O) energy level ratio

    if larger: insufficient oxygen

    if smaller: insufficient carbon

19. ground state energy level for ^{4}Helium (^{4}He)

    if larger: insufficient carbon and oxygen

    if smaller: insufficient carbon and oxygen

20. decay rate of ^{8}Beryllium (^{8}Be)

    if slower: heavy element fusion would generate catastrophic
        explosions in all the stars

    if faster: no element production beyond beryllium and, hence,
        no life chemistry possible

21. mass excess of the neutron over the proton

    if greater: neutron decay would leave too few neutrons to form
        the heavy elements essential for life

    if smaller: proton decay would cause all stars to collapse rapidly into
        neutron stars or black holes

22. initial excess of nucleons over anti-nucleons

    if greater: too much radiation for planets to form

    if smaller: not enough matter for galaxies or stars to form

23. polarity of the water molecule

    if greater: heat of fusion and vaporization would be too great for life to
        exist

    if smaller: heat of fusion and vaporization would be too small for life's
        existence; liquid water would become too inferior a solvent for life
        chemistry to proceed; ice would not float, leading to a runaway
        freeze-up

24. supernovae eruptions

    if too close: radiation would exterminate life on the planet

> *if too far:* not enough heavy element ashes for the formation of rocky
> planets
>
> *if too frequent:* life on the planet would be exterminated
>
> *if too infrequent:* not enough heavy element ashes for the formation of
> rocky planets
>
> *if too late:* life on the planet would be exterminated by radiation
>
> *if too soon:* not enough heavy element ashes for the formation of rocky
> planets

25. white dwarf binaries

> *if too few:* insufficient fluorine produced for life chemistry to proceed
>
> *if too many:* disruption of planetary orbits from stellar density;
> life on the planet would be exterminated
>
> *if too soon:* not enough heavy elements made for efficient fluorine
> production
>
> *if too late:* fluorine made too late for incorporation in proto-planet

26. ratio of exotic to ordinary matter

> *if smaller:* galaxies would not form
>
> *if larger:* universe would collapse before solar type stars could form

God and the Astronomers

The discovery of this degree of design in the universe is having a profound theological impact on astronomers. As we noted already, Hoyle concludes that "a superintellect has monkeyed with physics, as well as with chemistry and biology,"[14] and Davies has moved from promoting atheism[15] to conceding that "the laws [of physics] . . . seem themselves to be the product of exceedingly ingenious design."[16] He further testifies:

> [There] is for me powerful evidence that there is something
> going on behind it all. . . . It seems as though somebody has
> fine-tuned nature's numbers to make the Universe. . . . The
> impression of design is overwhelming.[17]

Astronomer George Greenstein, in his book The Symbiotic Universe, expressed these thoughts:

> As we survey all the evidence, the thought insistently arises
> that some supernatural agency—or, rather, Agency—must be
> involved. Is it possible that suddenly, without intending to,
> we have stumbled upon scientific proof of the existence of a
> Supreme Being? Was it God who stepped in and so providen-
> tially crafted the cosmos for our benefit?[18]

Tony Rothman, a theoretical physicist, in a popular-level article on the anthropic principle (the idea that the universe possesses narrowly defined characteristics that permit the possibility of a habitat for humans) concluded his essay with these words:

> The medieval theologian who gazed at the night sky through the eyes of Aristotle and saw angels moving the spheres in harmony has become the modern cosmologist who gazes at the same sky through the eyes of Einstein and sees the hand of God not in angels but in the constants of nature. . . . When confronted with the order and beauty of the universe and the strange coincidences of nature, it's very tempting to take the leap of faith from science into religion. I am sure many physicists want to. I only wish they would admit it.[19]

In a review article on the anthropic principle published in the journal *Nature*, cosmologists Bernard Carr and Martin Rees state in their summary: "Nature does exhibit remarkable coincidences and these do warrant some explanation."[20] Carr in a more recent article on the anthropic principle continues:

> One would have to conclude either that the features of the universe invoked in support of the Anthropic Principle are only coincidences or that the universe was indeed tailor-made for life. I will leave it to the theologians to ascertain the identity of the tailor![21]

Physicist Freeman Dyson concluded his treatment of the anthropic principle with, "The problem here is to try to formulate some statement of the ultimate purpose of the universe. In other words, the problem is to read the mind of God."[22] Vera Kistiakowsky, MIT physicist and past president of the Association of Women in Science, commented, "The exquisite order displayed by our scientific understanding of the physical world calls for the divine."[23] Arno Penzias, who shared the Nobel prize for physics for the discovery of the cosmic background radiation, remarked:

> Astronomy leads us to a unique event, a universe which was created out of nothing, one with the very delicate balance needed to provide exactly the conditions required to permit

life, and one which has an underlying (one might say "supernatural") plan.[24]

Years before communism's fall, Alexander Polyakov, a theoretician and fellow at Moscow's Landau Institute, declared:

We know that nature is described by the best of all possible mathematics because God created it. So there is a chance that the best of all possible mathematics will be created out of physicists' attempts to describe nature.[25]

China's famed astrophysicist Fang Li Zhi and his coauthor, physicist Li Shu Xian, recently wrote, "A question that has always been considered a topic of metaphysics or theology the creation of the universe has now become an area of active research in physics."[26]

In the 1992 film about Stephen Hawking, *A Brief History of Time*, Hawking's colleague, distinguished mathematician Roger Penrose, commented, "I would say the universe has a purpose. It's not there just somehow by chance."[27] Hawking and Penrose's colleague George Ellis made the following statement in a paper delivered at the Second Venice Conference on Cosmology and Philosophy:

Amazing fine tuning occurs in the laws that make this [complexity] possible. Realization of the complexity of what is accomplished makes it very difficult not to use the word "miraculous" without taking a stand as to the ontological status of that word.[28]

Cosmologist Edward Harrison makes this deduction:

Here is the cosmological proof of the existence of God—the design argument of Paley—updated and refurbished. The fine tuning of the universe provides prima facie evidence of deistic design. Take your choice: blind chance that requires multitudes of universes or design that requires only one. . . . Many scientists, when they admit their views, incline toward the teleological or design argument.[29]

Allan Sandage, winner of the Craoord prize in astronomy (equivalent to the Nobel prize), remarked, "I find it quite improbable that such order came out of chaos. There has to be some organizing principle.

God to me is a mystery but is the explanation for the miracle of existence, why there is something instead of nothing."[30] Robert Griffiths, who won the Heinemann prize in mathematical physics, observed, "If we need an atheist for a debate, I go to the philosophy department. The physics department isn't much use."[31] Perhaps astrophysicist Robert Jastrow, a self-proclaimed agnostic,[32] best described what has happened to his colleagues as they have measured the cosmos:

> For the scientist who has lived by his faith in the power of reason, the story ends like a bad dream. He has scaled the mountains of ignorance; he is about to conquer the highest peak; as he pulls himself over the final rock, he is greeted by a band of theologians who have been sitting there for centuries.[33]

In all my conversations with those who do research on the characteristics of the universe, and in all my readings of articles or books on the subject, not one person denies the conclusion that somehow the cosmos has been crafted to make it a fit habitat for life. Astronomers by nature tend to be independent and iconoclastic. If an opportunity for disagreement exists, they will seize it. But on the issue of the fine tuning or careful crafting of the cosmos, the evidence is so compelling that I have yet to hear of any dissent.

The Creator's Personality

Does the fine tuning imply purposeful design? So many parameters must be fine tuned and the degree of fine tuning is so high, no other conclusion seems possible.

As Harrison pointed out, the evidence permits only two options: divine design or blind chance. Blind chance, as we saw in chapter 12, is ruled out since conclusions based on chance must be derived from known, not hypothetical, sample sizes. The known sample size for the universe(s) is one and always will be only one since the space-time manifold for the universe is closed (meaning we humans cannot, even in principle, ever discover anything about others possibly existing).

Much more is going on, however, than mere talk by astronomers about the design of the cosmos for life support. Words such as *somebody fine tuned nature, superintellect, monkeyed, overwhelming design, miraculous, hand of God, ultimate purpose, God's mind, exquisite order, very delicate balance, exceedingly ingenious, supernatural Agency, supernatural plan, tailor-made, Supreme Being, and providentially crafted* obviously apply to a Person. Beyond just establishing that the Creator is a Person, the findings about design provide some evidence of what that Person is like.

One characteristic that stands out dramatically is His interest in and care for living things, particularly the human race. We see this care in the vastness and quality of the resources devoted to life support.

For example, the mass density of the universe, as huge as it is, focuses on the needs of humans. How? The mass density determines how efficiently nuclear fusion operates in the cosmos. The mass density we measure translates into about a hundred-billion-trillion stars for the presently observable universe. As table 14.1 indicates (page 118), if the mass density is too great, too much deuterium (an isotope of hydrogen with one proton and one neutron in the nucleus) is made in the first few minutes of the universe's existence. This extra deuterium will cause the stars to burn much too quickly and erratically for any of them to support a planet with life. On the other hand, if the mass density is too small, so little deuterium and helium are made in the first few minutes that the heavier elements necessary for life will never form in stars. What this means is that the approximately hundred-billion-trillion stars we observe in the universe—no more and no less—are needed for life to be possible in the universe. God invested heavily in living creatures. He constructed all these stars and carefully crafted them throughout the age of the universe so that at this brief moment in the history of the cosmos humans could exist and have a pleasant place to live.

Non-Theistic Responses

When it comes to the finely tuned characteristics of the universe, non-theists find themselves in a difficult spot. The evidence is too weighty and concrete to brush aside. The evidence is inanimate; so appeals to Darwinist hypotheses cannot be made. Appeals to near infinite time are thwarted by the proofs for time's creation only a few billion years ago. The following three arguments seem to cover the range of non-theistic replies to the evidence for cosmic design:

Argument 1: We would not be here to observe the universe unless the extremely unlikely did take place.

The evidence for design is merely coincidental. Our existence simply testifies that the extremely unlikely did, indeed, take place by chance. In other words, we would not be here to report on the characteristics of the universe unless chance produced these highly unlikely properties.

Rebuttal: This argument is fundamentally an appeal to infinite chances, which already has been answered (see chapter 12). Another response has been developed by philosopher Richard Swinburne[34] and summarized by another philosopher, William Lane Craig:

> Suppose a hundred sharpshooters are sent to execute a prisoner by firing squad, and the prisoner survives. The prisoner should not be surprised that he does not observe that he is dead. After all, if he were dead, he could not observe his death. Nonetheless, he should be surprised that he observes that he is alive.[35]

To extend Craig and Swinburne's argument, the prisoner could conclude, since he is alive, that all the sharpshooters missed by some extremely unlikely chance. He may wish to attribute his survival to an incredible bit of good luck, but he would be far more rational to conclude that the guns were loaded with blanks or that the sharpshooters all deliberately missed. Someone must have purposed he should live. Likewise, the rational conclusion to draw from the incredible fine tuning of the universe is that Someone purposed we should live.

Argument 2: The design of the universe is mere anthropomorphism.
American astrophysicist Joseph Silk in his latest effort to communicate the physics of big bang cosmology to lay people mocks the conclusion that the universe has been fine-tuned for the support of life. He compares the "silliness" of the design idea with the folly of a flea's assumption that the dog on which it feeds has been designed precisely for its benefit. The flea's error, he suggests, becomes all too apparent once the dog is outfitted with a flea collar.[36]

Silk's argument ignores some key issues. While the flea may be a little self-centered in assuming that the dog was designed exclusively for it, there's no reason to deny that the dog was designed for a purpose, or for several purposes. (The myth that life is strictly the product of accidental natural processes is addressed in chapter 16.) The flea collar may argue more strongly for design (e.g., population control) than for lack of it. More importantly, while we can imagine a wide range of hosts suitable for the support of the flea, each of them requires elements of design to facilitate the flea's survival. Though suitable hosts for the flea are relatively abundant, suitable universes for life are not. Astrophysicists have been unable to invent hypothetical universes significantly different from ours that could support human beings or for that matter any conceivable kind of physical, intelligent life.

Argument 3: Design arguments are outside the realm of science and, therefore, must be ignored.

The publications of the National Center for Science Education, among other anti-creationist groups, repeatedly assert that science is "empirically based and necessarily materialist; miracles cannot be allowed," and that "any theory with a supernatural foundation is not scientific."[37] Since the design arguments imply supernatural intervention, they can be justifiably ignored because they "cannot be considered scientific."[38]

Rebuttal: To affirm that science and theology are mutually exclusive may be convenient for materialists unwilling to defend their philosophy, but it is untenable. Science is rarely religiously neutral. Similarly, religious faith is rarely scientifically neutral. Both science and theology frequently address cause and effect and processes of development in the natural realm. Both science and theology deal with the origin of the universe, the solar system, life, and humankind.

When it comes to causes, developmental processes, and origins, two possibilities always exist: natural or supernatural. To dogmatically insist that supernatural answers must never be considered is equivalent to demanding that all human beings follow only one religion, the religion of atheistic materialism. I find it ironic that in the name of religious freedom certain science education proponents insist on ridding our teaching and research institutions of any faith that dares to compete with their own.

Argument 4: Order can come out of chaos.

The idea that under strictly natural conditions order can and will arise out of chaos was first proposed by David Hume nearly two hundred years ago. Recently it has been revived by chemist and Nobel Laureate Ilya Prigogine in his book *Order Out of Chaos*,[39] and popularized by the blockbuster movie *Jurassic Park*. Hume made the claim without any evidential support. Prigogine pointed to several chemical reactions in which order appears to arise from chaotic systems. *Jurassic Park* actually addresses a different subject, namely chaos theory and fuzzy logic.

The principle behind chaos theory and fuzzy logic is that in trying to predict the outcome or future state of exceptionally complex systems, the investigator is better off settling for approximate answers or conclusions at each step in the solution of a problem rather than exact answers or conclusions. The presumption of a natural self-ordering principle in chaotic systems arises from the fact that the more complex a system, the greater the opportunity for departures from thermodynamic equilibrium in small portions of the system (and the greater the difficulty in determining what the thermodynamic equilibrium states actually are). According to the second law of thermodynamics, entropy increases in all systems, but entropy can decrease (i.e., order can increase) in part of a system, providing an extra increase of entropy (i.e., disorder) occurs in a different part of the system. Because human investigators may be prone to underestimate the complexity of some systems, they occasionally are surprised by how far from thermodynamic equilibrium a small portion of a system can stray. However, the thermodynamic laws predict that these departures are temporary, and the greater the departure, the more rapidly the departures are corrected.

Without departures from thermodynamic equilibrium, raindrops and snowflakes, for example, would not form. But, raindrop and snowflake formation comes close to the self-ordering limits of natural process. Though snowflake patterns exhibit a high degree of order, their information content or level of design remains quite low. The distinction is roughly like the difference between the New Testament and a book containing the sentence "God is good" repeated 90,000 times. The latter shows considerable order but not much information. The former contains both a high degree or order and a high degree of information (or design). Prigogine's examples exhibit increases in order but without significant increases in information content. Natural processes cannot explain the exceptionally high level of design and information content in living organisms or in the structure of the universe that makes life possible.

Argument 5: As we continue to evolve, we will become the Creator-Designer.
In their book *The Anthropic Cosmological Principle*, astrophysicists John Barrow and Frank Tipler review many new evidences for the design of the universe.[40] They go on to discuss versions of the anthropic principle like WAP (weak anthropic principle: conscious beings can only exist in an environment with characteristics that allow for their habitation), SAP (strong anthropic principle: nature must take on those characteristics to admit somewhere, sometime the existence of conscious beings),

and more radical versions, including PAP (participatory anthropic principle: conscious observers are necessary to bring the universe into existence, and the universe is necessary to bring observers into existence). But what they favor is FAP (final anthropic principle).

With FAP, the life that exists (past, present, and future) will continue to evolve with the inanimate resources of the universe until it all reaches a state that Barrow and Tipler call the "Omega Point."[41] This Omega Point, they say, is an Entity that has the properties of omnipotence, omnipresence, and omniscience, with the capacity to create in the past.[42] In other words, the Creator-God does not exist yet, but we (all life and all inanimate structures in the universe) are gradually evolving into God. When God is thus finally constructed, His power will be such that He can create the entire universe with all of its characteristics of design billions of years ago.

In his latest book, *The Physics of Immortality*,[43] Tipler proposes that evolution toward the Omega Point will occur through advancing computer technology. By extrapolating computer capability doubling time (currently, about eighteen months) some millions of years into the future, Tipler predicts that a future generation of human beings will be able not only to alter the entire universe and all the laws of physics but also to create a God who does not yet exist. Furthermore, we will be able to resurrect every human being who has ever lived by recovering the memories that once resided in each person's brain.

Rebuttal: It is hard to treat these FAP and Omega Point hypotheses seriously. In the New York Review of Books, noted critic Martin Gardner offered this evaluation of Barrow and Tipler's work:

> What should we make of this quartet of WAP, SAP, PAP, and FAP? In my not so humble opinion I think the last principle is best called CRAP, the Completely Ridiculous Anthropic Principle.[44]

In *The Physics of Immortality* Tipler grossly overestimates the role of human memory and the future capability of computers. Just as computers cannot function with memory banks only, so, too, the human mind and human consciousness do not operate by memory alone. While remarkable advances in computer technology are taking place now, the laws of physics impose predictable finite limits on future computer hardware. As Roger Penrose has documented rigorously in *The Emperor's New Mind* and *Shadows of the Mind*, these limits do not even permit the duplication of human consciousness let alone the fantastic capabilities Tipler suggests.[45]

But Tipler apparently wants to alter much more than just the universe and the laws of physics. He believes, for example, that future computers will be able to expose people to game theory principles so effectively that all destructive thoughts and actions will be purged and villainy no longer occur, even for the likes of Adolf Hitler and Mata Hari.[46] In Tipler's religion, the redemptive work of a Savior becomes unnecessary. Consider, however, that if Tipler's proposal were true, the better people comprehend game theory, the less propensity they would exhibit to commit evil. Unfortunately for Tipler, no such correlation is in evidence.

Tipler not only banishes hell but also redesigns heaven. Tipler's "heaven" brings relational (more accurately, sexual) bliss to every man and woman. He produces an equation to "prove" that this computer generated cosmic utopia will bring a woman to every man and a man to every woman capable of delivering 100,000 times the impact and satisfaction of the most fulfilling partner each can imagine in life as we know it.[47] The popular appeal of such a notion documents the spiritual bankruptcy of our times. Evidently, many people have never tasted any greater delight than what sexual experience can bring.

In an article for the Skeptical Inquirer, Gardner again brandished his satiric knifes:

> I leave it to the reader to decide whether they should opt for OPT (Omega Point Theology) as a new scientific religion superior to Scientology—one destined to elevate Tipler to the rank of a prophet greater than L. Ron Hubbard—or opt for the view that OPT is a wild fantasy generated by too much reading of science fiction.[48]

In their persistent rejection of an eternal, transcendent Creator, some cosmologists (and others) are resorting to increasingly irrational options. There is a certain logic to it, however. If for personal or moral reasons the God of the Bible is unacceptable, then given all the evidence for transcendence and design, the alternatives are limited to flights of fancy.

Through time, as we unlock more of the secrets of the vast cosmos, men and women will be even more awed about how exquisitely designed the universe is. But where will that awe be aimed—at the created thing, or at the Creator? That is each person's choice.

CHAPTER FIFTEEN

EARTH: THE PLACE FOR LIFE

The mind boggles in trying to grasp the minute detail the Designer wove together to make the universe suitable for life. That same beautiful intricacy is apparent as one looks closer to home—at our galaxy, our sun, our neighboring planets, our earth, our moon, and more.

The first astronomers to provide evidence of these intricacies were Frank Drake, Carl Sagan, and Iosef Shklovskii. They developed the evidence out of their desire to estimate the number of planets in the universe with favorable environments for the support of life. By 1966 Shklovskii and Sagan had determined it takes a certain kind of star with a planet located at just the right distance from that star to provide the minimal conditions for life.[1] Working with just these two parameters, they estimated that 0.001% of all stars could have a planet capable of supporting advanced life.[2]

Much subsequent evidence has shown that Shklovskii and Sagan overestimated the range of permissible star types and the range of permissible planetary distances, and they also ignored dozens of other significant parameters. But their estimate of a million-plus possible life sites for our galaxy persisted. It is this optimistic estimate that has fueled the search for extraterrestrial intelligent life.

In addition to much private money, more than $100 million in U.S. taxpayer support had been devoted to the search for radio signals from extraterrestrial intelligent life.[3] With all the evidence for divine design (and against a naturalistic explanation) in the universe, one would think some caution (and some theology) would be in order before committing this much money. As we will see, the evidence for divine design mounts dramatically as we move from a large system, like the universe as a whole, to smaller systems such as our galaxy, our star, our planet, and life itself.

The Right Galaxy

Not all galaxies are created equal in terms of their capacity to support life. Popular media often give the impression that all galaxies are spirals like our Milky Way. Actually only 5% of the galaxies in the universe are spirals.[4] The other 95% are either elliptical or irregular.

In elliptical galaxies star formation ceases before the interstellar medium becomes enriched enough with heavy elements. For life, stellar systems need to form late enough that they can incorporate this heavy-element-enriched material.

The problem with large irregular galaxies is they have active nuclei. These nuclei spew out life-destroying radiation and material. Meanwhile most small irregular galaxies have insufficient quantities of the heavy elements essential for life.

Physicists R. E. Davies and R. H. Koch recently published a paper on the necessary cosmic conditions for the solar system to contain the elements essential for life.[5] Since the 1960s astronomers have realized the emerging solar system would need contact with exploded supernovae remains to possess sufficient heavy elements for rocky planets and life chemistry.

Davies and Koch estimate how many supernovae must erupt in our galaxy to produce the needed quantity of elements heavier than helium. The answer: an average of one every three years from the time our galaxy originated (about ten billion years ago). Since the present rate is less than one supernova every fifty years, the rate must have been extremely high in the early history of our galaxy.

This conclusion matches the results from the best astrophysical models and observations of star formation in our galaxy. It also matches the requirements for life. Supernovae must occur in great abundance early in the history of a galaxy to supply enough heavy element enrichment to allow a planet like Earth to form as early as it did.

It also is essential that the supernova event rate be relatively low in the present era. If it were not, the radiation from supernova eruptions would frequently exterminate life on Earth.

The frequency of supernova eruptions (per unit volume) is strongly dependent on location. The solar system must be positioned in the right part of the spiral arm, and that spiral arm must be at the right distance from the center of our galaxy.

But there is one life-essential heavy element that is not made by supernovae: fluorine. It is made in sufficient quantities only on relatively rare objects: the surfaces of white dwarf stars bound into binary systems with larger stellar companions. The larger star must orbit closely enough to the white dwarf that it loses significant material to the white dwarf. At the surface of the white dwarf, some of this material is converted to fluorine. Then the white dwarf must lose this fluoridated material to interstellar space for it to be incorporated into a future solar system. This sequence means that the universe, our galaxy, and the sun's position in our galaxy must assume narrowly specified characteristics if Earth is to obtain the fluorine it needs for the support of life.

The location, types, rates, and timings of both supernova events and white dwarf binaries severely constrains the possibility of finding a life support site. The vast majority of galaxies are eliminated from contention, and the vast majority of stars in the few remaining galaxies also are eliminated.

Another Kind of Life?

The significance of these findings is underscored by John Maddox, a member of the editorial board of *Nature* and a staunch opponent of theism, who attempted to find a way around Davies and Koch's implications for creation.[6] He suggested life need not be at all like terrestrial life as we know it. What support did he offer? None.

As physicist Robert Dicke observed thirty-two years ago, if you want physicists (or any other life forms), you must have carbon.[7] Boron and silicon are the only other elements on which complex molecules can be based, but boron is extremely rare, and silicon can hold together no more than about a hundred amino acids. Given the constraints of physics and chemistry, we can reasonably assume that life must be carbon-based.

Another sensitive characteristic of our galaxy for life support is stellar density. Most galaxies and all globular clusters (spherically symmetric systems of stars containing more than a hundred-thousand stars and residing around and in between galaxies) have stellar densities far too high for life-supportable planets. If the stars are too close to one another, their gravitational interactions with one another disrupt planetary orbits. On the other hand, the stars cannot be too far apart. If they are, the life-essential heavy elements residing in the interstellar medium will be too thinly distributed. This eliminates many dwarf and irregular galaxies from contention.The need for the right stellar density also means the sun's location is sensitive. A distance too close or far away from the center of a galaxy or too close or far away from the densest part of the spiral arm in which it resides would eliminate the possibility of a planet capable of supporting life.

The Right Star

Not only is a particular kind of galaxy essential for life, the star around which a life-bearing planet revolves must be just right. As we have seen, it must be located in the right part of the galaxy. It must also be a single star system. Zero or two-plus star systems will fail.

A planet ripped away from its star will be too cold for life. But if a planet is orbiting a binary or multiple star system, the extra star(s) frequently will pull its orbit out of the temperature zone essential for life support. Only about a fourth of the stars in our galaxy meet the criterion of being bachelor stars.

As Shklovskii and Sagan first pointed out, a life support planet must be maintained by a star of very specific mass. A star more massive than the sun will burn too quickly and too erratically for life on the planet to be sustained. But the star cannot be any less massive either. The smaller the mass of the star, the closer the planet must be to that star to maintain a temperature suitable for life chemistry. This causes a problem because the tidal interaction between a star and its planet increases dramatically as the distance separating them shrinks: Bringing the planet just the slightest bit closer causes such a tremendous increase in tidal interaction that the planet's rotation period quickly lengthens from hours to months. This is the fate, for example, of both Mercury and Venus.

The star must form at just the right time in the history of the galaxy. If it forms too soon or too late, the mix of heavy elements suitable for life chemistry will not exist. It is also essential that the star be middle-aged. Only middle-aged stars are in a sufficiently stable burning phase.

Even stars that are the most stable and in the most stable parts of their burning cycles experience changes in luminosity that can be detrimental for life. The sun's luminosity, for example, has increased by more than 35% since life was first introduced on Earth. Such a change is more than enough to exterminate life. But life survived on Earth because the increase in solar luminosity was exactly cancelled out each step of the way by a decrease in the efficiency of the greenhouse effect in Earth's atmosphere. This decrease in greenhouse efficiency arose through the careful introduction of just the right species of life in just the right quantities at just the right times. The slightest "evolutionary accident" would have caused either a runaway freeze-up or runaway boiling (see box on this page).

Here, the materialists offer no explanation. How could strictly natural Darwinist processes possibly have anticipated the physics of solar burning?

CLIMATIC RUNAWAYS

Earth's biosphere is poised between a runaway freeze-up and a runaway evaporation. If the mean temperature of the earth's surface cools by even a few degrees, more snow and ice than normal will form. Snow and ice reflect solar energy much more efficiently than other surface materials. The reflection of more solar energy translates into lower surface temperatures, which in turn cause more snow and ice to form and subsequently still lower temperatures.

If the mean temperature of the earth's surface warms just a few degrees, more water vapor and carbon dioxide collect in the atmosphere. This extra water vapor and carbon dioxide create a better greenhouse effect in the atmosphere. This in turn causes the surface temperature to rise again, which releases even more water vapor and carbon dioxide into the atmosphere resulting in still higher surface temperatures.

The Right Planet

As biochemists now concede, for life molecules to operate so that organisms can live requires an environment where liquid water is stable. This means that a planet cannot be too close to its star or too far away. In the case of planet Earth, a change in the distance from the sun as small as 2% would rid the planet of all life.[8]

The temperature of a planet and its surface gravity determine the escape velocity, a measure of which atmospheric gases dissipate to outer space and which are retained. For a planet to support life, it is essential for water vapor (molecular weight 18) to be retained while molecules as heavy as methane (molecular weight 16) and ammonia (molecular weight 17) dissipate. Therefore, a change in surface gravity or temperature of just a few percent will make the difference.

While planet Earth has just the right surface gravity and temperature,[9] ammonia and methane, in fact, disappear much faster than their escape velocities would indicate. The reason is that chemical conditions in Earth's upper atmosphere—also indicative of fine tuning—work efficiently to break down both molecules.[10]

Rotation and Life

The rotation period of a life-supporting planet cannot be changed by more than a few percent. If the planet takes too long to rotate, temperature differences between day and night will be too great. On the other hand, if the planet rotates too rapidly, wind velocities will rise to catastrophic levels. A quiet day on Jupiter (rotation period of ten hours), for example, generates thousand mph winds. Though our hurricanes and tornados are tough to endure, we are better off with their occasional blasts than we would be with more extreme differences between day and night temperatures.

Rotation periods of life-supportable planets, however, are not constant. Though Earth does not suffer catastrophic tidal interaction with the sun as Venus does, it still experiences enough that its rotation period is gradually braked. Every year, Earth's rotation period is slowed by a small fraction of a second. If the earth were much younger than its 4.6 billion years, it would be rotating too quickly for life. If it were much older, it would be rotating too slowly. Since primitive life can tolerate more rapid rotation than advanced life, life can and did survive being placed on Earth when Earth was only 0.8 billion years old.

In addition to the length of the rotation period, the rate of change in that period is also sensitive for life support. Each species that has existed throughout the earth's history has had a range of tolerable rotation periods and a range of tolerable change in that period. As it turns out, most of the species that have ever existed throughout the earth's history could not have survived if the earth's rotational slowing had been greater or lesser than a certain narrow range (roughly between two and four hours per day per billion years).

Two additional factors have been identified. One is that the more rapid rotation of Earth in the past decreased the size of weather systems (relative to the surface area they covered) and concentrated them along the equator.[11] The net result was that extra light and heat from the sun necessary at that time for life support did indeed reach the earth's surface. The other is that the percentage of the earth's surface area covered by water was greater in the past.[12] Volcanic activity and plate tectonics caused continents to rise and increase in area until the rate of erosion balanced the increase. Since water bodies absorb and retain heat far more effectively than land masses, the larger ocean area of the past contributed significantly to the warmth of the early Earth's climate.

Even tectonic plate activity (often expressed as earthquakes) is a sensitive parameter for life. Without earthquakes, nutrients essential for life on the continents would erode and accumulate in the oceans. However, if earthquake activity were too great, it would be impossible for humans to reside in cities. On Earth, the number and intensity of earthquakes is large enough to recycle life-essential nutrients back to the continents but not so intense that dwelling in cities is impossible.

The Right Planetary Companions

Late in 1993, planetary scientist George Wetherill, of the Carnegie Institution of Washington, D.C., made an exciting discovery about our solar system. In observing computer simulations of our solar system, he found that without a Jupiter-sized planet positioned just where it is, Earth would be struck about a thousand times more frequently than it is already by comets and comet debris.[13] In other words, without Jupiter, impacts such as the one that wiped out the dinosaurs would be common.[14]

Here is how the protection system works. Jupiter is two and a half times more massive than all the other planets combined. Because of its huge mass, thus huge gravity, and its location between the earth and the cloud of comets surrounding the solar system, Jupiter either draws comets (by gravity) to collide with itself, as it did in July 1994,[15] or, more commonly, it deflects comets (again by gravity) right out of the solar system. In Wetherill's words, if it were not for Jupiter, "we wouldn't be around to study the origin of the solar system."[16]

Neither would we be around if it were not for the very high regularity in the orbits of both Jupiter and Saturn. Also in July 1994, French astrophysicist Jacques Laskar determined that if the outer planets were less [orbitally] regular, then the inner planets' motions would be chaotic, and Earth would suffer orbital changes so extreme as to disrupt its climatic stability.[17] In other words, Earth's climate would be unsuitable for life. (As it is, the tiny variations in Jupiter and Saturn's orbits may someday but not soon bounce lightweight Mercury right out of the solar system.) Thus even the characteristics of Jupiter and Saturn's orbits must fit within certain narrowly defined ranges for life on Earth to be possible.

The Right Moon

The moon plays a critical role for life as well. Our moon is unique among solar system bodies in that it is so large relative to its planet. As a result, our moon exerts a significant gravitational pull on Earth. Thanks to this pull, coastal sea waters are cleansed and their nutrients replenished, also the obliquity (tilt of the rotation axis relative to the orbital plane) of Earth is stabilized (a critical factor for avoiding climatic extremes).[18] The moon in its formative stages probably contributed to the rapid removal of greenhouse gases from Earth, thereby saving the planet from the fate of Venus (runaway boiling, see "Climatic Runaways," page 135) and permitting large oceans to form.[19]

So we see that Earth is prepared for life through a variety of finely tuned characteristics of our galaxy, star, planet, and moon. This discussion by no means exhausts the list of characteristics that must be fine tuned for life to exist. The astronomical literature now includes discussions on more than forty different characteristics that must take on narrowly defined values. And this list grows longer with every new year of research. What was two parameters in 1966 grew to eight by the end of the '60s, to twenty-three by the end of the '70s, to thirty by the end of the '80s, to the current list of more than forty. A sampling of the parameters that must be fine tuned for the support of life is presented in table 15.1.

Table 15.1: Evidence for the Design of the Galaxy-Sun-Earth-Moon System for Life Support[20]

The following parameters of a planet, its moon, its star, and its galaxy must have values falling within narrowly defined ranges for life of any kind to exist. Characteristics 2 and 3 have been repeated from table 14.1 since these apply to both the universe and the galaxy.

   1. galaxy type
      if too elliptical: star formation would cease before sufficient heavy
         element build-up for life chemistry
      if too irregular: radiation exposure on occasion would be too severe and
         heavy elements for life chemistry would not be available

2. supernova eruptions

   if too close: life on the planet would be exterminated by radiation

   if too far: not enough heavy element ashes would exist for the
   formation of rocky planets

   if too frequent: life on the planet would be exterminated

   if too infrequent: not enough heavy element ashes would be
   present for the formation of rocky planets

   if too late: life on the planet would be exterminated by radiation

   if too soon: not enough heavy element ashes would exist for the
   formation of rocky planets

3. white dwarf binaries

   if too few: insufficient fluorine would be produced for life
   chemistry to proceed

   if too many: planetary orbits would be disrupted by stellar density;
   life on the planet would be exterminated

   if too soon: not enough heavy elements would be made for
   efficient fluorine production

   if too late: fluorine would be made too late for incorporation in
   protoplanet

4. parent star distance from center of galaxy

   if farther: quantity of heavy elements would be insufficient to
   make rocky planets

   if closer: galactic radiation would be too great; stellar density
   would disturb planetary orbits out of life support zones

5. number of stars in the planetary system

   if more than one: tidal interactions would disrupt planetary orbits

   if less than one: heat produced would be insufficient for life

6. parent star birth date

   if more recent: star would not yet have reached stable burning
   phase; stellar system would contain too many heavy elements

   if less recent: stellar system would not contain enough heavy elements

7. parent star age

   if older: luminosity of star would change too quickly

   if younger: luminosity of star would change too quickly

8. parent star mass

   if greater: luminosity of star would change too quickly;
   star would burn too rapidly

   if less: range of distances appropriate for life would be too narrow;
   tidal forces would disrupt the rotational period for a planet
   of the right distance; uv radiation would be inadequate
   for plants to make sugars and oxygen

9. parent star color

   if redder: photosynthetic response would be insufficient

if bluer: photosynthetic response would be insufficient
10. parent star luminosity relative to speciation
    if increases too soon: would develop runaway greenhouse effect
    if increases too late: would develop runaway glaciation
11. surface gravity (escape velocity)
    if stronger: planet's atmosphere would retain too much ammonia
        and methane
    if weaker: planet's atmosphere would lose too much water
12. distance from parent star
    if farther: planet would be too cool for a stable water cycle
    if closer: planet would be too warm for a stable water cycle
13. inclination of orbit
    if too great: temperature differences on the planet would be
        too extreme
14. orbital eccentricity
    if too great: seasonal temperature differences would be
        too extreme
15. axial tilt
    if greater: surface temperature differences would be too great
    if less: surface temperature differences would be too great
16. rotation period
    if longer: diurnal temperature differences would be too great
    if shorter: atmospheric wind velocities would be too great
17. rate of change in rotation period
    if larger: surface temperature range necessary for life
        would not be sustained
    if smaller: surface temperature range necessary for life
        would not be sustained
18. age
    if too young: planet would rotate too rapidly
    if too old: planet would rotate too slowly
19. magnetic field
    if stronger: electromagnetic storms would be too severe
    if weaker: ozone shield and life on the land would be inadequately
        protected from hard stellar and solar radiation
20. thickness of crust
    if thicker: too much oxygen would be transferred from
        the atmosphere to the crust
    if thinner: volcanic and tectonic activity would be too great
21. albedo (ratio of reflected light to total amount falling on surface)
    if greater: runaway glaciation would develop
    if less: runaway greenhouse effect would develop
22. collision rate with asteroids and comets

if greater: too many species would become extinct

if less: crust would be too depleted of materials essential for life

23. oxygen to nitrogen ratio in atmosphere

if larger: advanced life functions would proceed too quickly

if smaller: advanced life functions would proceed too slowly

24. carbon dioxide level in atmosphere

if greater: runaway greenhouse effect would develop

if less: plants would be unable to maintain efficient photo synthesis

25. water vapor level in atmosphere

if greater: runaway greenhouse effect would develop

if less: rainfall would be too meager for advanced life on the land

26. atmospheric electric discharge rate

if greater: too much fire destruction would occur

if less: too little nitrogen would be fixed in the atmosphere

27. ozone level in atmosphere

if greater: surface temperatures would be too low

if less: surface temperatures would be too high; there would be too much uv radiation at the surface

28. oxygen quantity in atmosphere

if greater: plants and hydrocarbons would burn up too easily

if less: advanced animals would have too little to breathe

29. tectonic plate activity

if greater: too many life forms would be destroyed

if less: nutrients on ocean floors (from river runoff) would not be recycled to the continents through tectonic uplift

30. oceans-to-continents ratio

if greater: diversity and complexity of life forms would be limited

if smaller: diversity and complexity of life forms would be limited

31. global distribution of continents (for Earth)

if too much in the southern hemisphere: seasonal temperature differences would be too severe for advanced life

32. soil mineralization

if too nutrient poor: diversity and complexity of life forms would be limited

if too nutrient rich: diversity and complexity of life forms would be limited

33. gravitational interaction with a moon

if greater: tidal effects on the oceans, atmosphere, and rotational period would be too severe

if less: orbital obliquity changes would cause climatic instabilities; movement of nutrients and life from the oceans to the continents and continents to the oceans would be insufficient; magnetic field would be too weak

Chances for Finding a Life Support Planet

Each of these thirty-three parameters must be within certain limits to avoid disturbing a planet's capacity to support life. For some, including many of the stellar parameters, the limits have been measured quite precisely. For others, including many of the planetary parameters, the limits are less precisely known. Trillions of stars are available for study, and star formation is quite well understood and observed. On the other hand, only nine planets can be studied, and though a fairly good theory of planetary formation is available, the details have yet to be worked out. Another problem is that planetary formation cannot be fully observed.

Let's look at how confining these limits can be. Among the least confining would be the inclination of a planet's orbit and the distribution of its continents. The limits for these are loose, eliminating only 20% of all candidates. More confining would be parameters such as the planet's rotation period and its albedo (see table 15.1, item 21, page 140), which eliminate about 90% of all candidates from contention. Most confining of all would be parameters such as the parent star's mass and the planet's distance from its parent star, which eliminate 99.9% of all candidates.

Of course, not all the listed parameters are strictly independent of the others. Dependency factors could reduce the degree of confinement. On the other hand, all these parameters must be kept within specific limits for the total time span needed to support life on a candidate planet. This increases the degree of confinement.

Not to Mention . . .

About a dozen more parameters, such as atmospheric transparency, pressure, and temperature gradient, other greenhouse gases, location of different gases and minerals, and mantle and core constituents and structures, currently are being researched for their sensitivity in supporting life. They involve greater complexities, however, than the parameters discussed here, and estimates of their sensitivity are much more difficult to determine. Nevertheless, it is possible, even at this stage in the research efforts, to gather many of the planetary system parameters for life support and determine a crude estimate for the possibility that by natural means alone there would exist a planet capable of supporting life.

An attempt at calculating the possibility of such a planet is presented in table 15.2 (page 143). Although I have tried to be conservative in assigning probabilities, I readily admit many of the estimates may need to be modified.

Future research should provide us with much more accurate probabilities. If past research is any indication, however, the number of parameters should increase and the probabilities decrease. Thus, with considerable security, we can draw the conclusion that much fewer than a trillionth of a trillionth of a trillionth of a trillionth of a percent of all stars could possibly possess, without divine intervention, a planet capable of sustaining advanced life. Considering that the observable universe contains less than a trillion galaxies, each averaging a hundred-billion stars, we can see that not even one planet would be expected, by natural processes alone, to possess the necessary conditions to sustain life (see box on page 144).

Table 15.2: An Estimate of the Probability for Attaining the Necessary Parameters for Life Support

Parameter	Probability that feature will fall in the required range
galaxy type	.1
star location	.2
number of stars in system	.2
star birth date	.2
star age	.4
star mass	.001
star luminosity relative to speciation	.0001
star color	.4
supernovae rates and locations	.01
white dwarf binary types, rates, and locations	.01
planetary distance from star	.001
inclination of planetary orbit	.8
axis tilt	.3
rotation period	.1
rate of change in rotation period	.05
orbit eccentricity	.3
surface gravity (escape velocity)	.001
tidal force	.1
magnetic field	.01
albedo	.1
density	.1
thickness of crust	.01

oceans to continents ratio	.2
rate of change in oceans to continents ratio	.1
global distribution of continents	.3
asteroidal and cometary collision rate	.1
rate of change in ast. and comet collision rate	.1
position and mass of Jupiter relative to Earth	.01
eccentricity and regularity of Jupiter and Saturn's orbits	.05
atmospheric transparency	.01
atmospheric pressure	.1
atmospheric electric discharge rate	.1
atmospheric temperature gradient	.01
carbon dioxide level in atmosphere	.01
oxygen quantity in atmosphere	.01
ozone quantity and location in atmosphere	.01
water vapor level in atmosphere	.01
oxygen to nitrogen ratio in atmosphere	.1
quantity of greenhouse gases in atmosphere	.01
soil mineralization	.1
seismic activity	.1
dependency factors	1,000,000,000.
longevity requirements	.0001

Probability for occurrence of all forty-one parameters = 10^{-53}
Maximum possible number of planets in universe = 10^{22}

Much less than one chance in a million trillion exists that even one such planet would occur anywhere in the universe

---

HOW MANY PLANETS?

Only nine planets have been detected in the universe. Perturbations (small disturbances) in the positions of several stars reveal the presence of other planet-sized bodies. Dusty disks have been observed to surround many young stellar objects. Such objects, unlike older stars, can draw on newly available heavy elements. Additional research indicates that only slowly rotating bachelor stars similar to the sun have the possibility of stable planets.

The conclusion? The universe probably contains no more than one planet for every thousand stars. An extreme upper limit would be an average of one planet per star.

These factors would seem to indicate that the galaxy, the sun, Jupiter, Saturn, the earth, and the moon, in addition to the universe, have undergone divine design. It seems apparent that personal intervention on the part of the Creator takes place not just at the origin of the universe but also much more recently. In other words, Earth seems more than simply "the pick of the litter," the planet selected from the Creator's searching through the vastness of the cosmos for life's best home. Rather, the remoteness of the probability of finding a planet fit for life suggests that the Creator personally and specially designed and constructed our galaxy, our sun, Jupiter, Saturn, the moon, and Earth for life.

If divine design is essential to explain the properties of simpler systems such as the universe, our galaxy, and the solar system, how much more necessary is God's involvement to explaining systems as complex as organisms, including human beings? As for the millions of dollars spent by the U.S. government on the search for extraterrestrial intelligence, former Senator William Proxmire may have said it best. We would be far wiser to spend the money looking for intelligent life in Washington.

CHAPTER SIXTEEN

BUILDING LIFE

In previous chapters we looked at some of the burgeoning evidence for divine design in the universe, our galaxy, our sun, our planet, and our moon. This glowing testimony to the work of the Designer pales, however, in comparison to the evidence that resides in living organisms.

For the universe and the solar system we noted some characteristics that must be fine tuned to better than one part in 10^{37} for life to be possible. But, the fine tunings necessary to build an independent, functioning organism require precision crafting such as people have never before imagined, precision to one part in a number so big that it would fill thousands of books to write out.

The Time Scale
When it comes to the origin of life, many biologists (and others) have typically assumed that plenty of time is available for natural processes to perform the necessary assembly. But discoveries about the universe and the solar system have shattered that assumption. What we see now is that life must have originated on Earth quickly.

In early 1992 Christopher Chyba and Carl Sagan published a review paper on the origins of life.[1] *Origins* is plural for a good reason. Research indicates that life began, was destroyed, and began again many times during that era before it finally took hold.

Fully formed cells show up in the fossil record as far back as 3.5 billion years, and limestone, formed from the remains of organisms, dates back 3.8 billion years. The ratio of ^{12}Carbon to ^{13}Carbon found in ancient sediments[2] also indicates a plenitude of life on Earth for the era between 3.5 and 3.8 billion years ago.

But that was an era of grave danger for life. Though the research is recent, it leaves no room for doubt (based on dating of lunar craters and on comparisons of craters on the moon, Mars, and Mercury) that Earth and other bodies close to the sun experienced heavy bombardment by meteors, comets, asteroids, and dust in their early history.[3] From 4.25 until 3.8 billion years ago, the bombardment of Earth was so intense that no life could have survived it. From 3.8 until 3.5 billion years ago the bombardment gradually decreased to its present comparatively low level. But during those 300 million years at least thirty life-exterminating impacts must have occurred. These findings have enormous significance to our theories about the origin of life. They show that life sprang up on Earth (and re-sprang) in what could be called geologic instants, periods of ten-million years or less (between devastating impacts).[4]

From the perspective of our life span, a ten-million-year window may seem long, but it is impossibly short to those seeking to explain life's origins without divine input.

Prebiotic Soups

Attempts to show that life can and does come together on its own have resulted in experiments with prebiotic soups (warm ponds enriched with life-building molecules). Even under the highly favorable conditions of a laboratory, these soups have failed to produce anything remotely resembling life. One problem is that they produce only a random distribution of left- and right-handed prebiotic molecules. (Many prebiotic molecules, notably all but one of the bioactive amino acids, occur in two mirror-image forms that are arbitrarily termed left- and right-handed.) Life chemistry demands that all the molecules be either right- or left-handed. With all our learning and technology we cannot even come close to bringing life together in the lab. How can we expect it to bring itself together in just a few million years in the chaotic world of nature?

Amazingly, Chyba and Sagan find hope in the extraterrestrial bombardment. Glossing over the destructive effects of the collisions, they hypothesize a possibly beneficial effect. They suggest that this extraterrestrial bombardment may have assisted life formation by delivering concentrated doses of prebiotic molecules. How reasonable is this suggestion? Though comets, meteorites partly composed of carbon, and interplanetary dust particles may carry some prebiotics, they carry far too few to make a difference. In fact, with every helpful molecule they may bring, come several more that would get in the way—useless molecules that would substitute for the needed ones. And again, the left- or right-handedness problem persists.

Atmosphere Problem

Chyba, Sagan, and others cling to yet another slim chance. They suggest that the atmospheric conditions 3.8 billion years ago might not have been too unfavorable for life. Perhaps the conditions were just neutral. Unfavorable in the context of life assembly is an "oxidizing" atmosphere, one in which atoms and molecules bond with oxygen atoms. Favorable would be a "reducing" atmosphere, one in which atoms and molecules bond with hydrogen rather than with oxygen atoms. Neutral, as Chyba and Sagan define it, would be an atmosphere that allows at least some hydrogen bonding. But this idea, too, reflects wishful thinking. Atmospheric physicists established more than five years ago that Earth's atmosphere has been fully oxidizing (enough free oxygen exists to oxidize organic compounds) for at least the last four billion years.[5]

Under oxidizing conditions, processes producing amino acids (protein building blocks) and nucleotides (DNA and RNA building blocks) operate 30 million times less efficiently than they would under reducing conditions.[6] Natural primordial soups would contain far too few prebiotic molecules to overcome this inefficiency, not to mention the destructive chemical processes. Worse yet, the minute amino acid production would almost entirely be composed of the simple acid, glycine.[7] The more complex acids that are also needed would be virtually missing.

The Odds

The problems of primordial soups are big, but bigger yet is the infeasibility of generating, without supernatural input, an enormous increase in complexity. A wide gulf separates an aqueous solution containing a few amino acids from the simplest living cell.

Years ago, molecular biophysicist Harold Morowitz calculated the size of this gulf. If one were to take the simplest living cell and break every chemical bond within it, the odds that the cell would reassemble under ideal natural conditions (the best possible chemical environment) would be one chance in $10^{100,000,000,000}$.[8] Most of us cannot even begin to picture a speck of chance so remote. Another way of depicting the assembly problem is schematically outlined in figure 16.1.

With odds as remote as 1 in $10^{100,000,000,000}$, the time scale issue becomes completely irrelevant. What does it matter if the Earth has been around for ten seconds, ten thousand years, or ten billion years? The size of the universe is of no consequence either. If all the matter in the visible universe were converted into the building blocks of life, and if assembly of these building blocks were attempted once a microsecond for the entire age of the universe, then instead of the odds being 1 in $10^{100,000,000,000}$, they would be 1 in $10^{99,999,999,916}$.

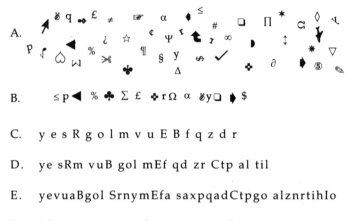

B.   ≤p◀ % ♣ Σ £ ◆rΩ α ♂y□ ♦ $

C.   y e s R g o l m v u E B f q z d r

D.   ye sRm vuB gol mEf qd zr Ctp al til

E.   yevuaBgol SrnymEfa saxpqadCtpgo alznrtihIo

F.   I love mango and papaya yoghurt.

Figure 16.1: An Analogy for Some of the Steps Needed in the Assembly of Life Molecules

Life molecules are composed of proteins and nucleic acids. The proteins, for example, are built from twenty distinct amino acids, nineteen of which must be oriented in a left-handed configuration. Moreover, most of these amino acids must be sequenced in a specific manner and to a specific length. In the natural world over eighty distinct amino acids exist, 50% right-handed and 50% left-handed. The problem for life assembly is to select from the randomly oriented amino acids only those that are correctly oriented (step A to B), then to select out only the life-specific amino acids (step B to C), then to bond the amino acids together into short chains (step C to D), then to bond the short chains together to make chains of the necessary lengths, typically, several hundred amino acids long (step D to E), and finally to select out those chains in the right order that have the amino acids in the proper sequences (step E to F). Meanwhile, the whole process must be protected so that the rate of formation remains sufficiently above the rate of destruction.

Non-Theists' Responses

Non-theists typically counter Morowitz' odds by pointing out that not every amino acid and nucleotide must be strictly sequenced for life molecules to function. They are right, and thus the probability for reassembly improves. But Morowitz also assumed that all the amino acids were bioactive. In fact, only twenty of the more than eighty naturally occurring amino acids are bioactive, and only those that are left-handed can be used. So the probability declines again. Furthermore, Morowitz assumed totally favorable conditions, only constructive chemical processes operating. Under natural circumstances, destructive chemical processes operate at least as frequently as constructive chemical processes. The bottom line is the odds for the assembly of the simplest living entity actually grow worse as more details are figured into the calculation.

Another attempt to wiggle out is to suggest that the simplest living entity 3.5 billion years ago was far simpler than what exists today. The difficulty here is that conditions on Earth 3.5 billion years ago were not enough different from conditions today to warrant such an idea. In fact, conditions were so similar that if life were spontaneously generating 3.5 billion years ago, we could expect to see it doing so today. Minimum complexity presents another problem. Organisms below a certain level of complexity cannot survive independently. As Morowitz demonstrated, this minimum complexity is not much below what we see in organisms today.

Finally, as astronomer Michael Hart demonstrated in 1982, even if you grant non-theists their wildest scenario concerning the origin of life, it still fails:

> Let us suppose (very optimistically) that in a strand of genesis DNA there are no fewer than 400 positions where any one of the four nucleotide residues will do, and at each of 100 other positions either of two different nucleotides will be equally effective, leaving only 100 positions which must be filled by exactly the right nucleotides. This appears to be an unrealistically optimistic set of assumptions; but even so, the probability that an arbitrarily chosen strand of nucleic acid could function as genesis DNA is only one in 10^{90}. Even in 10 billion years, the chance of forming such a strand spontaneously would be only 10^{-90} times 10^{60}, or 10^{-30}. . . . For each of 100 different specific genes [the minimum needed] to be formed

spontaneously (in ten billion years) the probability is $(10^{-30})^{100}$ = 10^{-3000}. For them to be formed at the same time, and in close proximity, the probability is very much lower.[9]

For those who want the most realistic calculation of the odds of life assembly under natural conditions, the papers[10] and book[11] by information theorist Hubert Yockey are excellent.

New Hope in RNA?

A smattering of papers published recently in Science momentarily lifted non-theistic biologists' mood of despair. Those papers discussed what seemed a possible way around some of the complexities of life.[12] Here's the background.

Molecules responsible for life chemistry cannot function by themselves. DNA (molecules that hold the blueprints for the construction of life molecules), proteins (molecules that follow portions of the blueprints in building and repairing life molecules), and RNA (molecules that carry the blueprints from the DNA to specific proteins) are all interdependent.

Thus, for life to originate mechanistically, all three kinds of molecules would need to emerge spontaneously and simultaneously from inorganic compounds. Even the most optimistic of researchers agreed that the chance appearance of these incredibly complex molecules at exactly the same time and place was beyond the realm of natural possibility.

However, in 1987 an experiment demonstrated that one kind of RNA can act as an enzyme or catalyst (an agent to facilitate a chemical process). It can function like a protein, at least to a limited degree.[13] This finding led to some leaps of faith. Since it was assumed already that RNA could be more easily constructed under prebiotic conditions than DNA or proteins, the suggestion arose that a primitive RNA molecule—capable of functioning as a protein and as DNA—evolved by natural means out of a primordial soup. In time, this "primitive" RNA was said to specialize, evolving into the three kinds of molecules we now recognize as RNA, DNA, and proteins.

The discoveries reported a few months ago showed yet more protein-like capabilities of RNA molecules. A research group presented evidence that a certain RNA molecule could stimulate two amino acids to join together with a peptide bond (the kind of chemical bond formed in proteins).[14] A second research team observed another RNA molecule both making and breaking the bonds that join amino acids to RNA.[15] Though these capabilities plus the ones observed earlier add up to only a tiny fraction of all the functions proteins perform, several origin-of-life theorists now are proposing that no proteins were necessary for the first life forms.

These new findings may seem to make "easier" the origin of life by strictly natural processes, but that is not necessarily the case. Even if a single primordial molecule could perform all the functions of modern DNA, RNA, and proteins, such a molecule would have to be no less complex in its information content (i.e., its built-in "knowledge" of what to do) than the sum of modern DNA, RNA, and proteins. In other words, the task of assembling such an incredibly versatile molecule is no easier than assembling the three different kinds of molecules. The information content of the three is simply concentrated into one enormously complex molecule. Even Leslie Orgel, a leading proponent of an RNA origin of life, admitted, "You have to get an awful lot of things right and nothing wrong."[16]

Another catch in these arguments is the false notion that RNA is easier to assemble than proteins or DNA. For twenty years researchers and texts taught that RNA had been synthesized in a lab under prebiotic conditions. This myth was exploded by Robert Shapiro at a meeting of the International Society for the Study of the Origin of Life held at Berkeley in 1986. Some three hundred of the top origin-of-life researchers from around the world were present.

Shapiro traced all the references to RNA synthesis back to one ambiguous paper published in 1967. At the same meeting he went on to demonstrate that the synthesis of RNA under prebiotic conditions is essentially impossible. No one at the meeting challenged the soundness of his conclusion. Shapiro then published his case against RNA synthesis in the journal Origins of Life and Evolution of the Biosphere,[17] a case that remains unchallenged to this day.[18]

Error-Handling Capability

Proteins and nucleic acids demonstrate a considerable tolerance for substitutions of alternative amino acids and nucleotides at certain sites. This has led to some questioning of their divine design. But as we saw in chapter 14, life cannot possibly exist in the universe unless several sources of radiation exist at highly specified levels. These radiation sources inevitably will cause some breakdown or changes in the structures of life molecules. Therefore, it is essential for life molecules to be so designed that they can still function even after suffering some limited destruction.

One useful analogy for visualizing the error-handling capability of proteins and nucleic acids would be computer programs. Consider a computer program with a million lines of code which, in spite of the random destruction of ten thousand lines of code, still performs its intended function. No one has written such an error-tolerant program. It could be done, but the task would be orders of magnitude more difficult than writing a program where the programer need not worry about random destruction of his code. Likewise, the tolerance for substitutions in life molecules should drive us toward, not away from, the conclusion of divine design.

Life on Mars?

Though I'm convinced that the origin of life defies a naturalistic explanation, I am expecting that life, or the remains of life, will eventually be discovered on Mars. My reason has nothing to do with spontaneous generation. It has everything to do with Mars' proximity to Earth.

In 1989, on ABC's "Nightline" with Ted Koppel, two astronomers and a science journalist declared that the discovery of life on Mars would provide virtual proof that life does indeed originate and evolve, and quite easily, by natural processes. Here is their line of reasoning: So far, we know of life's existence on only one planet orbiting one star out of ten-billion-trillion stars in the cosmos. If life is found on Mars, we would know it exists on two planets, but not just any two planets, two planets orbiting the same star. Instead of just one life site out of ten-billion-trillion candidates, we would have two life sites out of nine (the nine planets of our solar system). Such a finding would suggest that life is abundant throughout our universe, abundant by spontaneous generation.

By their faulty reasoning and failure to acknowledge relevant data, these influential men are setting their audience up for a deception. The remains, at least, of many micro-organisms are likely to be found on Mars for no other reason than that Mars is only thirty-five-million miles away from Earth. In other words, these zealous evolutionists, bent on searching for life on Mars, seem to ignore important facts about the transportability and survivability of Earth life forms. Consider the following data:[19]

1. Balloon missions flown in the 1960s found an abundance of microbial life at altitudes ranging from 30,000 to 130,000 feet.
2. The solar wind is capable of wafting tiny life forms (sizes ranging from 0.2 microns to about 1 micron) outward through the solar system and perhaps beyond.
3. Many micro-organisms can be kept at liquid air temperatures (about –200° degree Centigrade) for more than six months without losing their capacity to germinate.
4. Several microbial species exposed for five days to the vacuum conditions of outer space did not lose their viability.
5. Some microbes are capable of absorbing 600 kilorads of x-ray radiation without losing their viability.
6. Even very tiny amounts of graphite (of which there is more than an adequate supply in outer space) will protect micro-organisms from harmful ultraviolet radiation.
7. Meteorites large enough to make a crater greater than 60 miles across will cause Earth rocks to escape Earth's gravity. Out of 1,000 such rocks ejected, 291 strike Venus, 20 go to Mercury, 17 hit Mars, 14 make it to Jupiter, and 1 goes all the way to Saturn. Traveling the distance with these rocks will be many varieties of Earth life.

Thus there are many reasons to believe that millions of Earth's minute creatures have been deposited on the surface of Mars and other solar system planets.

Admittedly, conditions on Mars are unfavorable for the germination of such life except for only the briefest of moments. A liquid drop of water on the Martian surface, for example, evaporates in less than a second. Thus, living "adult" organisms should be quite rare on Mars. But, we should not be surprised to find considerable quantities of spores and the remains of biological material.

The discovery of microbial life and creatures perhaps as large as nematodes on Mars—a discovery we can expect as technology continues to advance—will probably be touted as proof of naturalistic evolution, when in truth it proves nothing of the kind. It will prove something, however, about the amazing vitality of what God created.

For Further Study
Because outstanding work done by specialists is available on the origin of life, I have limited my discussion here to a brief review. For

those who want more, I recommend *Origins* by Robert Shapiro (a non-theist),[20] *Information Theory and Molecular Biology* by Hubert Yockey (an agnostic),[21] and *The Mystery of Life's Origin* by Charles Thaxton, Walter Bradley, and Roger Olsen (all professing Christians).[22]

Universal Revelation

Wherever we look in the realm of nature, we see evidence for God's design and exquisite care for His creatures. Whether we examine the cosmos on its largest scale or its tiniest, His handiwork is evident. Whether we work in disciplines where simplicity and rigor predominate (for example, mathematics, astronomy, and physics) or in disciplines where complexity and information predominate (for example, biochemistry, botany, and zoology), God's fingerprints are visible.

Because of the quickening pace of technology and scientific research, the picture of God's attributes available to us through nature grows clearer. Further, since all the nations and cultures of the world are gaining scientific knowledge and technological competence, this testimony to God through nature is reaching out to all the peoples of the earth, paving the way for a surge of response to the gospel of Jesus Christ proclaimed by human messengers. Referring to God's revelation through the heavens, the Apostle Paul stated:

> Their sound has gone out to all the earth, and their words to the ends of the world.[23]

CHAPTER SEVENTEEN

EXTRA-DIMENSIONAL POWER

As we have seen in previous chapters, the recent measurings of the cosmos have revealed not only the existence of God but also His transcendence, His personality, and even His care and love for human beings. These discoveries lead to some important conclusions about the awesome power available to God and consequently the extent of His ability to bless humankind.

Because human beings can visualize phenomena only in dimensions that they can experience, in their attempts to describe God, they characterize Him as a Being confined to a four-dimensional box. One reason we know the Bible comes from a supernatural source is that, just like the implications from the recent measurings of the cosmos, it claims that God is not so confined—He transcends the space-time continuum of the universe. In its unique insistence that God moves and operates in dimensions independent of length, width, height, and time, the Bible not only insists on extra-dimensional capacities for God, but it also specifically describes how He functions in these extra dimensions (see table 10.1, page 78).

The Bible is unique, too, in describing certain attributes of God, such as the Trinity—in which God is depicted simultaneously as one, two, and three. It also portrays God as predetermining everything for us while simultaneously giving us freedom of choice. These concepts are provable contradictions in four dimensions, but each can be resolved when eight or more space-time dimensions or their equivalent are taken into consideration. Let us examine the Trinity as a specific example.

The Trinity: An Absurdity?

Ironically, adherents of nonChristian religions—like Islam and the

Jehovah's Witnesses—often appeal to limited dimensionality as a proof against Christianity. Often I have encountered apologists from such faiths who state categorically Christianity is false since the Trinity is mathematically absurd.

My initial response is to agree. The Trinity is a mathematical absurdity in the context of just the four dimensions of length, width, height, and time. Then I share with them the evidence from general relativity, the big bang, and particle physics for the existence of several more dimensions of space and time besides the four we humans experience. In particle physics, for example, all workable theories for the unification of the four fundamental forces of physics require that a minimum of nine dimensions of space and time must have existed in the first 10^{-34} seconds following the creation event.[1] Since God controls all these dimensions, He must be able to fully operate in them all. In fact, who is to say that He does not operate in spiritual dimensions completely distinct from space and time?

Given all this extra-dimensional capacity, it is fairly easy to demonstrate (but not visualize) that the Trinity becomes mathematically feasible.

We'll begin with a simple example of an extra dimension transforming a contradiction into a resolved paradox: In two dimensions in which only length and width exist, triangles can never be equal to circles. Triangles have three corners and circles have none. But in three dimensions of length, width, and height, a triangle could be flipped up on its base so that the third corner resides above the base in the dimension of height. Then the triangle could be rotated on its base so as to transcribe the shape of a cone. Also, a cone is a series of concentric circles ending at a point (the third corner of the triangle). Thus, in three dimensions of space, it is possible in one context for a triangle to be a circle and in another context (such as on a piece of paper) for a triangle not to be a circle. Therefore, one could conclude that in three spatial dimensions triangles can simultaneously be circles and not be circles.

In the same manner, a few extra dimensions of space and a few more of time would make possible the existence of God as a Trinity, an Entity who is simultaneously singular and plural. Such demonstrations of extra-dimensional resolutions of several aspects of the Trinity are currently available, but are beyond the limitations of this brief review.[2] What can be considered, however, is how extra dimensions elucidate some of the ways the Triune God relates to us.

Nearness of God

The Bible declares forthrightly that God is very close to each and every one of us.[3] But, it just as forthrightly states that God is invisible.[4] The Apostle Paul says that no one has ever seen God, nor can see Him.[5] Evidently, it is impossible for us humans to make physical contact with God. How, then, can God be so close and yet be beyond physical contact?

An analogy that might help was developed partly by Edwin Abbott, a nineteenth-century schoolmaster and preacher who published the book *Flatland: A Romance of Many Dimensions* in 1884.[6] Imagine a universe where only two dimensions of space exist rather than three. In such a universe, flatlanders would be confined to a plane of length and width with no possibility of operating in the dimension of height. A three-dimensional being then could approach the plane of the flatlanders and place his hand just a tenth of a millimeter above the two-dimensional bodies of two flatlanders separated from one another by just one centimeter. Since the three-dimensional being is slightly above the plane of the flatlanders, there is no possibility that the flatlanders can see him. And yet, the three dimensional being is a hundred times closer to each of the flatlanders than they are to one another.

As with the flatlanders, so it is with human beings. God is closer to each of us than we ever can be to one another. But because God's proximity to us takes place in dimensions we cannot tangibly experience, we cannot possibly see Him.

The only way we could see God is if He were to place a portion of His being into our dimensional realm. This would be analogous to the three-dimensional being poking his finger through the plane of the flatlanders. If one of the flatlanders were to investigate, he would draw the conclusion that this visitor to their realm is a small circle. But what if the three-dimensional being were to reveal separately to the friend of that flatlander three of his fingers? The friend then would draw the conclusion that the visitor to their realm was not one small circle but rather three small circles. We could then imagine a theological debate between the two flatlanders that would end up with the first flatlander founding the Church of the One Circle while the second would establish the Church of the Three Circles.

This analogy may appear amusing, but it fairly represents what nonChristians have done with the Trinity or Tri-Unity of God. Some have accepted God's singularity but rejected His plurality while others accept His plurality and reject His singularity. Only Christians accept that God is simultaneously singular and plural.

Power of God

It is easy to visualize how much more powerful and capable a three-dimensional being is compared to a two-dimensional being. But this is just one dimension of advantage. God has many dimensions of advantage over us both in space and in time (and perhaps in spiritual dimensions that are independent of space and time). Certain biblical doctrines, for example, the atonement of Christ, eternal security, and the simultaneity of freedom of human choice and divine predetermination, indicate a minimum of three time dimensions, or the equivalent, for God.[7]

Consider this one example of what is possible in three time dimensions. If God operated on a globe or sphere of time, the universe and all humanity could be confined to say a line on the sphere's equator. God, from a single point of time at the sphere's north pole, then, could drop perpendicular time lines to both our past and our future, simultaneously affecting both.

This illustration helps us to grasp a little of what happens when two extra dimensions of time are added. It boggles the mind to try to conceive of what can happen in seven more dimensions of space and time than what we humans can experience. But some inkling of what is possible in God's extra-dimensional realm is found in the New Testament.

Good That He Goes Away?

Just hours before Jesus was arrested by His enemies to be crucified, He told His disciples that He would be leaving them.[8] He informed them that He would be returning to His Father. As He said these things, His disciples' hearts were filled with sorrow.[9] It's easy to understand their feelings but not so easy to understand His words of reassurance: "It is for your good that I am going away."[10]

How could Jesus' going away be good? And how does this statement fit with His promise to be with them always? Paul's letter to the Philippians sheds some light:

> [Christ Jesus], being in very nature God, did not consider
> equality with God something to be grasped, but made him-
> self nothing, taking the very nature of a servant, being made

in human likeness. And being found in appearance as a man, he humbled himself and became obedient to death—even death on a cross! Therefore God exalted him to the highest place and gave him the name that is above every name.[11]

Jesus Christ was fully God, sharing in all the power, all the authority, and all the extra-dimensional capabilities God possesses. But for our sake, Christ lowered Himself and accepted the weakness and limitations of a human. He came into our dimensions to show us God, whom we could never otherwise picture, to give us an example of humility, and to pay the price for our redemption. After fulfilling His purpose in coming, Jesus once again took up all the power, authority, and extra-dimensional capacities that were rightfully His as God.

It is easy to empathize with the disciples' grief. Who would want to give up the tangible nearness of Jesus, seeing His face, hearing His words, feeling His touch, walking at His side? But as a human, Jesus could be in only one place at a time, holding one conversation at a time, performing one miracle at a time, etc. He needed rest, too.

Imagine all that we could gain by giving up His physical presence and regaining His extra-dimensional nearness. As He told His disciples, they would do greater miracles than the ones He had performed in front of them.[12] Further, He would never leave them, never fall asleep on them, never walk away to take care of someone else's need.[13] He could live in them, as well as beside them. The same powerful promise is made to every person who gives his or her life to Christ.

CHAPTER EIGHTEEN

THE POINT

Recently I spoke at a prestigious American university to a group of about forty science professors. I presented much of the information that appears in the pages of this book. Afterward, I conversed with four physics professors and asked for their response.

One of the four said he could not deny the truth of my message. The others nodded in agreement. I asked if they could see, then, the rationality of turning over their lives to Jesus Christ. Another of the four spoke up, saying, yes, they could see it, but they weren't yet ready to be that rational.

This statement was not a brush-off. Each man went on to name his reasons for resistance. One confessed his unwillingness to give up sexual immorality. The others spoke of deep wounds inflicted long ago by people who called themselves Christians. What each of them needed and showed willingness to receive was compassion—not to mention further dialogue.

Other professors expressed their need for more time to assimilate the information, to check references, and to investigate the Bible for themselves. I could empathize. After all, it took me two years of study to become willing to entrust my life to God's care and keeping (see chapter 2).

The beauty of the scientific (and other) evidences God has allowed us to discover about Him is that these meet the needs of two large segments of society: (1) those whose barriers to personal faith in Christ are intellectual, barriers of misinformation and misunderstanding, and (2) those whose barriers to faith come from personal pain or stubborn rebellion lurking under the cover of intellectual objections.

Drawing Near to God

It is awesome and wonderful to behold the character of the Creator in what He has made, but not everyone seems to see it. In the elegant architecture of the universe, a galaxy, the sun, the planets, the earth, the moon, a human being, or even the simplest living thing, some people are struck by the wisdom, power, and care of the Creator, while others see an amazing coincidence or the work of some unidentified extraterrestrials.

The book of Hebrews declares, "Anyone who comes to [God] must believe that he exists and that he rewards those who earnestly seek him."[1] In a sense, this verse sets forth a test of the heart. The person who wants to draw near to God must be (and will be) humble-hearted enough not only to see and accept His existence but also to see and trust His goodness, His love.

Israel's King David said, "The LORD is close to the broken-hearted," and "The LORD is near to all who call on him, to all who call on him in truth."[2]

Drawing near to God, calling on Him "in truth," begins with humbly acknowledging *who we are*—His creation and no one else's, foolishly inclined to place ourselves or others in God's place of authority over our lives—and *who He is*—the Divine Maker and Provider of all things, including a way across the gulf that divides us from Him.

Nature itself shows us these truths. But the Bible brings us the details and clarifies specifically how God bridges that gulf to bring us to Himself in a personal, everlasting relationship.

His care for us and desire to draw us near are best demonstrated in Christ's coming to Earth to pay the death penalty for our rebellious nature. The Bible says that we "who once were far away have been brought near through the blood of Christ."[3]

The way has been made, it has been made clear, and it has been proven by the resurrection of Jesus Christ—a testable fact of history.[4] But knowing the way and knowing God are not one and the same thing.

The crucial difference lies in our moving beyond acceptance of facts to acceptance of Him. Acceptance of His life in exchange for ours, of His death in exchange for ours, of His goodness in exchange for ours, of His authority in exchange for ours, even of His faithfulness in exchange for ours—this will be our step toward Him. The Bible assures us that if we draw near to Him, He will draw near to us.[5]

Why Extra Evidence to This Generation?

One question I hear often is, "Why has our generation been singled out to receive such an abundance of evidences for God and His Word?" Why have we been given so much more proof than previous generations?

The answer I see from the Bible is that God measures out evidence in direct proportion to the level of resistance to His truth. Where the resistance is relatively low, less hard evidence for the God of the Bible is necessary to overcome it. But where resistance, namely arrogance, is high, so also is the quantity and quality of evidence He provides to overcome it.

Let's consider our world, especially the Western world. We have the most wealth, the most discretionary time, the most education, and the most technology of any previous generation. And how do we respond to these blessings? The loudest voices say that we humans deserve all the credit. The loudest voices say that humanity is deity. Given such arrogance, no wonder evidences are being flooded upon us.

Though the opposition seems great, God has equipped us to overcome it. He says, "See, I have placed before you an open door that no one can shut."[6] Let's make good use of these evidences to build our own faith and the faith of others while He is holding that door open.

NOTES

ONE—*The Awe-Inspiring Night Sky*

1. George Roche, *A World Without Heroes: The Modern Tragedy* (Hillsdale, MI: Hillsdale College Press, 1987), page 120.
2. E. L. Schücking, "Cosmology," *Relativity Theory and Astrophysics 1. Relativity and Cosmology*, ed. Jurgen Ehlers (Providence, RI: American Mathematical Society, 1967), page 218.

TWO—*My Skeptical Inquiry*

1. The details of this calculation are presented in a short paper by the author called *Fulfilled Prophecy: Evidence for the Reliability of the Bible* (P. O. Box 5978, Pasadena, CA: Reasons To Believe, 1975).
2. A detailed account of my personal search for truth is given on an audiotape, *A Scientist Who Looked and Was Found* (Pasadena, CA: Reasons To Believe, 1988).

THREE—*The Discovery of the Century*

1. Nigel Hawkes, "Hunt On for Dark Secret of Universe," *London Times*, 25 April 1992, page 1.
2. Hawkes, page 1.
3. The Associated Press, "U.S. Scientists Find a 'Holy Grail': Ripples at Edge of the Universe," *International Herald Tribune* (London), 24 April 1992, page 1.
4. The Associated Press, page 1.
5. Thomas H. Maugh II, "Relics of 'Big Bang' Seen for First Time," *Los Angeles Times*, 24 April 1992, pages A1, A30.
6. David Briggs, "Science, Religion, Are Discovering Commonality in Big Bang Theory," *Los Angeles Times*, 2 May 1992, pages B6-B7.
7. Stephen Strauss, "An Innocent's Guide to the Big Bang Theory: Fingerprint in Space Left by the Universe as a Baby Still Has Doubters Hurling Stones," *The Globe and Mail* (Toronto), 25 April 1992, page 1.
8. Richard C. Tolman, "Thermodynamic Treatment of the Possible Formation of Helium from Hydrogen," *Journal of the American Chemical Society* 44 (1922), pages 1902-1908.
9. George Gamow, "Expanding Universe and the Origin of the Elements," *Physical Review* 70 (1946), pages 572-573.
10. Ralph A. Alpher and Robert C. Herman, "Evolution of the Universe," *Nature* 162 (1948), pages 774-775.
11. Arno A. Penzias and Robert W. Wilson, "A Measurement of Excess Antenna Temperature at 4080 Mc/s," *Astrophysical Journal* 142 (1965), pages 419-421; Robert H. Dicke et al., "Cosmic Black-Body Radiation," *Astrophysical Journal* 142 (1965), pages 414-419.
12. George F. Smoot, "Comments and Summary on the Cosmic Background Radiation," *Proceedings of the International Astronomical Union Symposium, No. 104: Early Evolution of the Universe and Its Present Structure*, ed. G. O. Abell and G. Chincarini (Dordrecht, Holland; Boston, MA, USA: Reidel Publishing, 1983), pages 153-158.

13. Craig J. Hogan, "Experimental Triumph," *Nature* 344 (1990), pages 107-108; J. C. Mather et al., "A Preliminary Measurement of the Cosmic Microwave Background Spectrum by the Cosmic Background Explorer (COBE) Satellite," *Astrophysical Journal Letters* 354 (1990), pages L37-L40.

14. Hugh Ross, *The Fingerprint of God*, 2nd ed. rev. (Orange, CA: Promise Publishing, 1991), pages 87-88.

15. Ross, page 124.

16. George F. Smoot et al., "Structure in the COBE Differential Microwave Radiometer First-Year Maps," *Astrophysical Journal Letters* 396 (1992), pages L1-L6; C. L. Bennett et al., "Preliminary Separation of Galactic and Cosmic Microwave Emission for the COBE Differential Microwave Radiometers," *Astrophysical Journal Letters* 396 (1992), pages L7-L12.

17. E. L. Wright et al., "Interpretation of the Cosmic Microwave Background Radiation Anisotropy Detected by the COBE Differential Microwave Radiometer," *Astrophysical Journal Letters* 396 (1992), pages L13-L18.

18. Geoffrey Burbidge's comments were made on a radio talk show called Live From LA with host Phil Reid on KKLA in Los Angeles, CA. The program aired 11 May 1992 and included comments on the big bang ripples discovery from Drs. G. De Amici, Geoffrey Burbidge, Russell Humphreys, and Hugh Ross.

19. Ron Cowen, "Balloon Survey Backs COBE Cosmos Map," *Science News* 142 (1992), page 420.

20. S. Hancock, et al., "Direct Observation of Structure in the Cosmic Background Radiation," *Nature* 367 (1994), pages 333-338.

21. A.C. Clapp, et al., "Measurements of Anistropy in the Cosmic Microwave Background Radiation at Degree Angular Scales Near the Stars Sigma Herculis and Iota Draconis," *Astrophysical Journal Letters* 433 (1994), pages L57-L60.

22. Ron Cowen, "COBE: A Match Made in Heaven," *Science News* 143 (1993), page 43; J.C. Mather, et al., "Measurement of the Cosmic Microwave Background Spectrum by the COBE FIRAS Instrument," *Astrophysical Journal* 420 (1994), pages 439-444.

23. Katherine C. Roth, David M. Meyer, and Isabel Hawkins, "Interstellar Cyanogen and the Temperature of the Cosmic Microwave Background Radiation," *Astrophysical Journal* 413 (1993), pages L67-L71.

24. Antoinette Songaila, et al., "Measurement of the Microwave Background Temperature at Redshift 1.776," *Nature* 371 (1994), pages 43-45.

25. David M. Meyer, "A Distant Space Thermometer," *Nature* 371 (1994), page 13.

26. Yuri I. Izotov, Trinh X. Thuan, and Valentin A. Lipovetsky, "The Primordial Helium Abundance from a New Sample of Metal-Deficient Blue Compact Galaxies," *Astrophysical Journal* 435 (1994), pages 647-667.

27. P. Jokobsen, et al., "Detection of Intergalactic Ionized Helium Absorption in a High-Redshift Quasar," *Nature* 370 (1994), pages 35-39; Antoinette Songaila, et al., "Deuterium Abundance and Background Radiation Temperature in High-Redshift Primordial Clouds," *Nature* 368 (1994), pages 599-604.

28. Yuri I. Izotov, Trinh X. Thuan, and Valentin A. Lipovetsky, pages 647-667.

FOUR—*The Matter Mystery*

1. Virginia Trimble, "Existence and Nature of Dark Matter in the Universe," *Frontiers in Physics, The Early Universe: Reprints*, ed. Edward W. Kolb and Michael S. Turner (Redwood City, CA: Addison-Wesley, The Advance Book Program, 1988), pages 97-99.

FIVE—*The Beautiful Fit*

1. Edward W. Kolb and Michael S. Turner, ed., *Frontiers in Physics, The Early Universe* (Redwood City, CA: Addison-Wesley, The Advance Book Program, 1990), pages 100-101.

2. Ron Cowen, "Hubble: A Universe Without End," *Science News* 141 (1992), page 79.

3. A. Songaila, et al., "Deuterium Abundance and Background Radiation Temperature in High-Redshift Primordial Clouds," *Nature* 368 (1994), page 599-600.

4. Peter Coles and George Ellis, "The Case for an Open Universe," *Nature* 370 (1994),

pages 609-613; P.J.E. Peebles, *Principles of Physical Cosmology* (Princeton, NJ: Princeton University Press, 1993), pages 475-483.

5. Peter Coles and George Ellis, page 609; P.J.E. Peebles, pages 475-477.

6. C. Alcock, et al., "Possible Gravitational Microlensing of a Star in the Large Magellanic Cloud," *Nature* 365 (1993), pages 621-623; E. Aubourg, et al., "Evidence for Gravitational Microlensing by Dark Objects in the Galactic Halo," *Nature* 365 (1993), pages 623-625; M. Della Valle, "Spectroscopic Observations of the Mt. Stromlo MACHO Candidate," *Astronomy and Astrophysics* 287 (1994), pages L31-L33; Ph. Jetzer, "On the Mass of the Dark Compact Objects in the Galactic Disk," CERN and Zurich University preprint, August 1994.

7. John Travis, "Massive Problem of Missing Dwarfs," *Science* 266 (1994), pages 1319-1320; Ron Cowen, "Hubble Finds Dark Matter Still a Mystery," *Science News* 146 (1994), page 357.

8. Penny D. Sackett, et al., "A Faint Luminous Halo That May Trace the Dark Matter Around Spiral Galaxy NGC 5907," *Nature* 370 (1994), pages 441-443.

9. Ron Cowen, "Boring into an Ancient Star," *Science News* 141 (1992), page 79; B. E. J. Pagel, "Beryllium and the Big Bang," *Nature* 354 (1991), pages 267-268.

10. Douglas K. Duncan, David L. Lambert, and Michael Lemke, "The Abundance of Boron in Three Halo Stars," *Astrophysical Journal* 401 (1992), pages 584-595.

11. C.C. Counselman III, et al., "Solar Gravitational Deflection of Radio Waves Measured by Very-Long Baseline Interferometry," *Physical Review Letters* 33 (1974), pages 1621-1623; R.D. Reasenberg, et al., "Viking Relativity Experiment: Verification of Signal Retardation by Solar Gravity," *Astrophysical Journal Letters* 234 (1979), pages 219-221.

12. David H. Roberts et al., "The Hubble Constant from VLA Measurement of the Time Delay in the Double Quasar 0957+561," *Nature* 352 (1991), pages 43-45; D. L. Jauncey, et al., "An Unusually Strong Einstein Ring in the Radio Source PKS 1830-211," *Nature* 352 (1991), pages 132-134; Ron Cowen, "And a Search for Dark Matter," *Science News* 141 (1992), page 79; I. Peterson, "Gravity Lenses for Peering into Darkness," *Science News* 141 (1992), page 293; Ron Cowen, "Quasar Hunt Bags Unusual Quarry," *Science News* 141 (1992), pages 410-411; Ron Cowen, "Gravity's Lens: Hubble Gets Sharpest Image," *Science News* 142 (1992), pages 260-261.

13. Cowen, "Gravity's Lens," pages 260-261.

14. Cowen, "And a Search for Dark Matter," page 79.

15. Cowen, "Gravity's Lens," pages 260-261; Edwin D. Loh and Earl J. Spillar, "A Measurement of the Mass Density of the Universe," *Astrophysical Journal Letters* 307 (1986), pages L1-L4.

16. Allan R. Sandage et al., "The Cepheid Distance to IC 4182: Calibration of M_V(max) for SN Ia 1937C and the Value of H_O," *Astrophysical Journal Letters* 401 (1992), pages L7-L10; Bertram Schwarzschild, "Supernova Distance Measurements Suggest an Older, Larger Universe," *Physics Today* (November 1992), pages 17-20.

17. Schwarzschild, pages 17-20; Savid Lindley, "A Distant Candle," *Nature* 360 (1992), page 413.

18. Sandage, et al., page L7. See also note added in proof on page L10.

19. Hugh Ross, *The Fingerprint of God*, 2nd ed. rev. (Orange, CA: Promise Publishing, 1991), pages 89-93; Rosie Wyse, "Oldest Stars Are Older Still," *Nature* 361 (1993), pages 204-205.

20. Peter Coles and George Ellis, pages 609-613; P.J.E. Peebles, pages 475-483.

21. Ron Cowen, "ROSAT Data Hint at a Closed Universe," *Science News* 143 (1993), page 20; Joseph Silk, "Dark Matter Comes in from the Cold," *Nature* 361 (1993), page 111.

22. Cowen, "ROSAT Data Hint at a Closed Universe," page 20; Richard J. Gott III, et al., "An Unbound Universe," *Astrophysical Journal* 194 (1974), pages 543-553.

23. Ron Cowen, "Nearby Galaxy Sheds Light on Dark Matter," *Science News* 143 (1993), pages 374-375; Faye Flam, "Spinning in the Dark," *Science* 260 (1993), page 1593.

24. Ann Finkbeiner, "The Quest for the Youngest Galaxies," *Science* 262 (1993), pages 1969-1970.

25. E. L. Wright, et al., "Interpretation of the Cosmic Microwave Background Radiation Anisotropy Detected by the COBE Differential Microwave Radiometer,"

Astrophysical Journal Letters 396 (1992), pages L13-L18; Francesco Lucchin, Sabino Matarrese, and Silvia Mollerach, "The Gravitational Wave Contribution to Cosmic Microwave Background Anisotropies and the Amplitude of Mass Fluctuations from COBE Results," *Astrophysical Journal Letters* 401 (1992), pages L49-L52; Toby Falk, Rachavan Rangarajan, and Mary Srednicki, "The Angular Dependence of the Three-Point Correlation Function of the Cosmic Microwave Background Radiation As Predicted by Inflationary Cosmologies," *Astrophysical Journal Letters* 403 (1993), pages L1-L3; Craig J. Hogan, "COBE Anisotropy from Supercluster Gas," *Astrophysical Journal Letters* 398 (1992), pages L77-L80; A. Kashlinsky, "Latest COBE Results, Large-Scale Structure Data, and Predictions of Inflation," *Astrophysical Journal Letters* 399 (1992), pages L1-L4; David P. Bennett, Albert Stebbins, and Francois R. Bouchet, "The Implications of the COBE Diffuse Microwave Radiation Results for Cosmic Strings," *Astrophysical Journal Letters* 399 (1992), pages L5-L8; Renyue Cen, et al., "A Tilted Cold Dark Matter Cosmological Scenario," *Astrophysical Journal Letters* 399 (1992), pages L11-L14; Yasushi Suto, "Three-Point Correlation Functions and the Hierarchical Clustering ANSATZ in Low-Density Cold Dark Matter Universes," *Astrophysical Journal Letters* 404 (1993), pages L1-L4; Chung-Pei Ma and Edmund Bertschinger, "Do Galactic Systems Form Too Late in Cold + Hot Dark Matter Models?" *Astrophysical Journal Letters*, 434 (1994), pages L5-L9.

26. Coles and Ellis, pages 609-614; David Coulson, et al., "Microwave Anistropies from Cosmic Defects," *Nature* 368 (1994), pages 27-31; Ben Moore, "Evidence Against Dissipationless Dark Matter from Observations of Galaxy Haloes," *Nature* 370 (1994), pages 629-631; Stefan Gottlober, Jan P. Mucket, and Alexei A. Starobinsky, "Confrontation of a Double Inflationary Cosmological Model with Observations," *Astrophysical Journal* 434 (1994), pages 417-423; Marc Kamionkowski, et al., "Cosmic Background Radiation Anistropy in an Open Inflation Cold Dark Matter Cosmogony," *Astrophysical Journal Letters* 434 (1994), pages L1-L4; Bharat Ratra and P.J. E. Peebles, "Cold Dark Matter Cosmogony in an Open Universe," *Astrophysical Journal Letters* 432 (1994), pages L5-L9.

SIX—*Einstein's Challenge*

1. Immanuel Kant, "Universal Natural History and Theory of the Heavens," *Theories of the Universe*, ed. Milton K. Munitz (Glencoe, IL: Free Press, 1957), page 240.

2. Rudolf Thiel, *And There Was Light: The Discovery of the Universe* (New York: Alfred A. Knopf, 1957), page 218; John Herman Randall, Jr., *The Career of Philosophy*, vol. 2 (New York: Columbia University Press, 1965), page 113; Kant, "Universal Natural History and Theory of the Heavens," pages 242-247.

3. Hugh Ross, *The Fingerprint of God*, 2nd ed. rev. (Orange, CA: Promise Publishing, 1991), pages 27-38.

4. Albert Einstein, "Zur Elektrodynamik bewegter Körper," *Annalen der Physik* 17 (1905), pages 891-921 [Hendrik A. Lorentz, et al., *The Principle of Relativity*, with notes by Arnold Sommerfeld, trans. W. Perrett and G. B. Jeffrey (London: Methuen and Co., 1923), pages 35-65]; Albert Einstein, "Ist die Trägheit eines Körpers von seinem Energieinhalt abhängig?" *Annalen der Physik* 18 (1905), pages 639-644 [Lorentz, et al., *The Principle of Relativity*, pages 67-71].

5. Robert Martin Eisberg, *Fundamentals of Modern Physics* (New York: John Wiley & Sons, 1961), pages 37-38, 75-76, 580-592; John D. Jackson, *Classical Electrodynamics* (New York: John Wiley and Sons, 1962), pages 352-369; S. K. Lamoreaux, et al., "New Limits on Spatial Anisotropy from Optically Pumped ^{201}Hg and ^{199}Hg," *Physical Review Letters* 57 (1986), pages 3125-3128. This recent experiment confirms the predictions of special relativity to better than one part in 10^{21}.

6. Albert Einstein, "Die Feldgleichungen der Gravitation," *Sitzungsberichte der Königlich Preussischen Akademie der Wissenschaften*, 25 November 1915, pages 844-847 (the following reference includes this reference); Albert Einstein, "Die Grundlage der allgemeinen Relativitätstheorie," *Annalen der Physik* 49 (1916), pages 769-822 [Lorentz, et al., *The Principle of Relativity*, pages 109-164].

7. Einstein, "Die Grundlage der allgemeinen Relativitätstheorie," pages 769-822

[Lorentz, et al., pages 109-164].

8. A. Vibert Douglas, "Forty Minutes with Einstein," *Journal of the Royal Astronomical Society of Canada* 50 (1956), page 100.

9. Lincoln Barnett, *The Universe and Dr. Einstein* (New York: William Sloane Associates, 1948), page 106.

10. Edwin Hubble, "A Relation Between Distance and Radial Velocity Among Extra-Galactic Nebulae," *Proceedings of the National Academy of Sciences* 15 (1929), pages 168-173.

11. Albert Einstein, *Out of My Later Years* (New York: Philosophical Library, 1950), page 27.

12. I have prepared a number of resources addressing the paradoxes of God's predetermination and man's free choice and the existence of evil and suffering in the presence of God's love and power. These range from brief papers to a chapter in my book *The Fingerprint of God*, to audiotape courses, to a video series prepared for television. These items are all available from Reasons To Believe, P. O. Box 5978, Pasadena, CA 91117.

SEVEN—Closing Loopholes: Round One

1. Arthur S. Eddington, "The End of the World: From the Standpoint of Mathematical Physics," *Nature* 127 (1931), page 450.

2. Arthur S. Eddington, "On the Instability of Einstein's Spherical World," *Monthly Notices of the Royal Astronomical Society* 90 (1930), page 672.

3. Hugh Ross, *The Fingerprint of God*, 2nd ed. rev. (Orange, CA: Promise Publishing, 1991), pages 89-93, 141-160.

4. Hugh Ross, *Creation and Time*, (Colorado Springs, CO: NavPress, 1994).

5. Hubert P. Yockey, "On the Information Content of Cytochrome c," *Journal of Theoretical Biology* 67 (1977), pages 345-376; Hubert P. Yockey, "Self Organization Origin of Life Scenarios and Information Theory," *Journal of Theoretical Biology* 91 (1981), pages 13-31; James A. Lake, "Evolving Ribosome Structure: Domains in Archaebacteria, Eubacteria, Eocytes, and Eukaryotes," *Annual Review of Biochemistry* 54 (1985), pages 507-530; M. J. Dufton, "Genetic Code Redundancy and the Evolutionary Stability of Protein Secondary Structure," *Journal of Theoretical Biology* 116 (1985), pages 343-348; Hubert P. Yockey, "Do Overlapping Genes Violate Molecular Biology and the Theory of Evolution?" *Journal of Theoretical Biology* 80 (1979), pages 21-26; John Abelson, "RNA Processing and the Intervening Sequence Problem," *Annual Review of Biochemistry* 48 (1979), pages 1035-1069; Ralph T. Hinegardner and Joseph Engleberg, "Rationale for a Universal Genetic Code," *Science* 142 (1963), pages 1083-1085; Hans Neurath, "Protein Structure and Enzyme Action," *Reviews of Modern Physics* 31 (1959), pages 185-190; Fred Hoyle and Chandra Wickramasinghe, *Evolution from Space* (New York: Simon and Schuster, 1981), pages 14-97; Charles B. Thaxton, Walter L. Bradley, and Roger Olsen, *The Mystery of Life's Origin* (New York: Philosophical Library, 1984); Robert Shapiro, *Origins* (New York: Summit Books, 1986), pages 117-131; Hugh Ross, *Genesis One: A Scientific Perspective*, 2nd ed. rev. (Pasadena, CA: Reasons To Believe, 1983), pages 9-10; Hubert P. Yockey, "A Calculation of the Probability of Spontaneous Biogenesis by Information Theory," *Journal of Theoretical Biology* 67 (1977), pages 377-398; W. W. Duley, "Evidence Against Biological Grains in the Interstellar Medium," *Quarterly Journal of the Royal Astronomical Society* 25 (1984), pages 109-113; Randall A. Kok, John A. Taylor, and Walter L. Bradley, "A Statistical Examination of Self-Ordering of Amino Acids in Proteins," *Origins of Life and Evolution of the Biosphere* 18 (1988), pages 135-142; John D. Barrow and Frank J. Tipler, *The Anthropic Cosmological Principle* (New York: Oxford University Press, 1986), pages 560-570; Hubert P. Yockey, *Information Theory and Molecular Biology* (Cambridge, U.K.: Cambridge University Press, 1992), pages 131-309.

6. Herman Bondi and T. Gold, "The Steady-State Theory of the Expanding Universe," *Monthly Notices of the Royal Astronomical Society* 108 (1948), pages 252-270; Fred Hoyle, "A New Model for the Expanding Universe," *Monthly Notices of the Royal*

Astronomical Society 108 (1948), pages 372-382.

7. Herman Bondi, *Cosmology*, 2nd ed. rev. (Cambridge, U.K.: Cambridge University Press, 1960), page 140; Hoyle, "A New Model for the Expanding Universe," page 372.

8. Fred Hoyle, *The Nature of the Universe*, 2nd ed. rev. (Oxford, U.K.: Basil Blackwell, 1952), page 111; Fred Hoyle, "The Universe: Past and Present Reflections," *Annual Reviews of Astronomy and Astrophysics* 20 (1982), page 3.

9. Ross, *The Fingerprint of God*, pages 81-96; J.C. Mather, et al., "Measurement of the Cosmic Microwave Background Spectrum by the COBE FIRAS Instrument," *Astrophysical Journal* 420 (1994), pages 439-444; Alan Dressler, et al., "New Images of the Distant, Rich Cluster CL 0939+4713 with WFPC2," *Astrophysical Journal Letters* 435 (1994), pages L23-L26.

10. Sir James H. Jeans, *Astronomy and Cosmogony*, 2nd ed. rev. (Cambridge, U.K.: Cambridge University Press, 1929), pages 421-422.

11. Thomas L. Swihart, *Astrophysics and Stellar Astronomy* (New York: John Wiley & Sons, 1968), pages 157-158.

12. Donald Hamilton, "The Spectral Evolution of Galaxies. I. An Observational Approach," *Astrophysical Journal* 297 (1985), pages 371-389.

13. Ross, *The Fingerprint of God*, pages 81-96; J.C. Mather, et al., pages 439-444; Dressler, et al., pages L23-L26.

14. Paul S. Wesson, "Olber's Paradox and the Spectral Intensity of the Extragalactic Background Light," *Astrophysical Journal* 367, 1 February 1991, pages 399-406.

15. One of the more spectacular evidences for the universe maturing with time was a recently announced Hubble Space Telescope discovery (Mark A. Stein, "Hubble's Galaxy Photos Show Universe in Flux," *Los Angeles Times*, 2 December 1992, pages B1, B4). A team led by astronomer Alan Dressler found that for a galaxy cluster four billion light years away (and hence four billion years younger than ours) the ratio of younger (spiral shaped) galaxies to older galaxies (elliptical shaped) was about six times higher than for our own galaxy cluster. For more details see my article, "Galaxy Formation Supports Creation," *Facts & Faith*, the Quarterly Newsletter of Reasons To Believe, Spring 1993, pages 2-3. For a list of references to additional evidences for the evolution of the universe see *The Fingerprint of God*, pages 81-82, 93-94.

16. John Gribbin, "Oscillating Universe Bounces Back," *Nature* 259 (1976), pages 15-16.

EIGHT—Closing Loopholes: Round Two

1. Robert H. Dicke, et al., "Cosmic Black-Body Radiation," *Astrophysical Journal Letters* 142 (1965), page 415.

2. Dicke, et al., page 414-415.

3. Richard J. Gott III, et al., "An Unbound Universe?" *Astrophysical Journal* 194 (1974), pages 543-553; Hyron Spinrad and S. Djorgovski, "The Status of the Hubble Diagram in 1986," *Observational Cosmology*, Proceedings of the 124th Symposium of the International Astronomical Union, held in Beijing, China, 25-30 August 1986, ed. A. Hewitt, G. Burbidge, and L. Z. Fang (Dordrecht, Holland; Boston, MA, USA: Reidel Publishing, 1987), pages 129-141; Paul J. Steinhardt, "Inflation and the Ω-Problem," *Nature* 345 (1990), pages 47-49; P.J.E. Peebles, "The Mean Mass Density of the Universe," *Nature* 321 (1986), pages 27-32; Donald Hamilton, "The Spectral Evolution of Galaxies. I. An Observational Approach," *Astrophysical Journal* 297 (1985), pages 371-389; Allan Sandage and G. A. Tammann, "The Dynamical Parameters of the Universe: H_0, q_0, Ω, $\wedge$, and K," *Large-Scale Structure of the Universe, Cosmology, and Fundamental Physics*, proceedings of the First ESO-CERN Symposium, 21-25 November 1983, ed. G. Setti and L. van Hove (Geneva: CERN, 1984), pages 127-149; J. Yang, et al., "Primordial Nucleosynthesis: A Critical Comparison of Theory and Observation," *Astrophysical Journal* 281 (1984), pages 493-511; Juan M. Uson and David T. Wilkinson, "Improved Limits on Small-Scale Anisotropy in Cosmic Microwave Background," *Nature* 312 (1984), pages 427-429; George F. R. Ellis, "Does Inflation Necessarily Imply $\Omega = 1$?" *Classical and Quantum Gravity* 5 (1988), pages 891-901.

4. Peter Coles and George Ellis, "The Case for an Open Universe," *Nature* 370 (1994),

pages 609-613; Craig J. Hogan, "Cosmological Conflict," *Nature* 371 (1994), pages 374-375; P.J.E. Peebles, Principles of Physical Cosmology (Princeton, NJ: Princeton University Press, 1993), pages 475-483.

5. Alan H. Guth and Marc Sher, "The Impossibility of a Bouncing Universe," *Nature* 302 (1983), pages 505-507; Sidney A. Bludman, "Thermodynamics and the End of a Closed Universe," *Nature* 308 (1984), pages 319-322.

6. Igor D. Novikov and Yakob B. Zel'dovich, "Physical Processes Near Cosmological Singularities," *Annual Review of Astronomy and Astrophysics* 11 (1973), pages 387-412.

7. Arnold E. Sikkema and Werner Israel, "Black-hole Mergers and Mass Inflation in a Bouncing Universe," *Nature* 349 (1991), pages 45-47.

8. André Linde, "Self-Reproducing Universe," lecture given at the Centennial Symposium on Large Scale Structure, California Institute of Technology, Pasadena, CA, 27 September 1991.

9. Linde, "Self-Reproducing Universe."

10. Charles W. Misner, Kip S. Thorne, and John Archibald Wheeler, *Gravitation* (San Francisco, CA: W. H. Freeman, 1973), page 752.

NINE—Science Discovers Time Before Time

1. Eric J. Lerner, *The Big Bang Never Happened* (New York: Random House, 1991), pages 120, 295-318.

2. Lerner, pages 7-8.

3. Lerner, pages 283-291, 300-301.

4. Hugh Ross, *The Fingerprint of God*, 2nd ed. rev. (Orange, CA: Promise Publishing, 1991), pages 53-68, 111-118.

5. Roger Penrose, "An Analysis of the Structure of Space-time," *Adams Prize Essay*, Cambridge University (1966); Stephen W. Hawking, "Singularities and the Geometry of Space-time," *Adams Prize Essay*, Cambridge University (1966); Stephen W. Hawking and George F. R. Ellis, "The Cosmic Black-Body Radiation and the Existence of Singularities in Our Universe," *Astrophysical Journal* 152 (1968), pages 25-36; Stephen Hawking and Roger Penrose, "The Singularities of Gravitational Collapse and Cosmology," *Proceedings of the Royal Society of London*, series A, 314 (1970), pages 529-548.

6. Hawking and Penrose, pages 529-548.

7. John Boslough, "Inside the Mind of a Genius," *Reader's Digest* (February 1984), page 120.

8. Albert Einstein, "Die Feldgleichungen der Gravitation," *Sitzungsberichte der Königlich Preussischen Akademie der Wissenschaften*, 25 November 1915, pages 844-847; Albert Einstein, "Die Grundlage der allgemeinen Relativitätstheorie," *Annalen der Physik* 49 (1916), pages 769-822 [Hendrik A. Lorentz, et al., *The Principle of Relativity*, with notes by Arnold Sommerfeld, trans. W. Perrett and G. B. Jeffrey (London: Methuen, 1923), pages 109-164]; Albert Einstein, "Erklärung der Perihelbewegung des Merkur aus der allgemeinen Relativitätstheorie," *Sitzungsberichte der Königlich Preussis-chenAkademie der Wissenschaften*, 18 November 1915, pages 831-839.

9. F. W. Dyson, Arthur S. Eddington, and C. Davidson, "A Determination of the Deflection of Light by the Sun's Gravitational Field, from Observations Made at the Total Eclipse of May 29, 1919," *Philosophical Transactions of the Royal Society of London*, series A, 220 (1920), pages 291-333.

10. Steven Weinberg, *Gravitation and Cosmology: Principles and Applications of the General Theory of Relativity* (New York: J. Wiley and Sons, 1972), page 198; Irwin I. Shapiro et al., "Mercury's Perihelion Advance: Determination by Radar," *Physical Review Letters* 28 (1972), pages 1594-1597; R. V. Pound and J. L. Snider, "Effect of Gravity on Nuclear Resonance," *Physical Review Letters* 13 (1964), pages 539-540.

11. C. Brans and Robert H. Dicke, "Mach's Principle and a Relativistic Theory of Gravitation," *Physical Review* 124 (1961), pages 925-935; J. W. Moffat, "Consequences of a New Experimental Determination of the Quadrupole Moment of the Sun for Gravitation Theory," *Physical Review Letters* 50 (1983), pages 709-712; George F. R. Ellis, "Alternatives to the Big Bang," *Annual Reviews of Astronomy and Astrophysics* 22

(1984), pages 157-184.

12. Irwin I. Shapiro, Charles C. Counselman III, and Robert W. King, "Verification of the Principle of Equivalence for Massive Bodies," *Physical Review Letters* 36 (1976), pages 555-558.

13. R. D. Reasenberg, et al., "Viking Relativity Experiment: Verification of Signal Retardation by Solar Gravity," *Astrophysical Journal Letters* 234 (1979), pages 219-221.

14. R. F. C. Vessot et al., "Test of Relativistic Gravitation with a Space- Borne Hydrogen Maser," *Physical Review Letters* 45 (1980), pages 2081-2084.

15. J. H. Taylor, "Gravitational Radiation and the Binary Pulsar," *Proceedings of the Second Marcel Grossman Meeting on General Relativity*, part A, ed. Remo Ruffini (Amsterdam: North-Holland Publishing, 1982), pages 15-19.

16. J. H. Taylor, et al., "Experimental Constraints on Strong-field Relativistic Gravity," *Nature* 355 (1992), pages 132-136.

17. Roger Penrose, *Shadows of the Mind: A Search for the Missing Science of Consciousness* (New York: Oxford University Press, 1994), page 230.

18. Alexander Vilenkin, "Did the Universe Have a Beginning?" *CALT-68-1772 DOE Research and Development Report*, California Institute of Technology, Pasadena, CA (November 1992).

19. Paul Davies, *God and the New Physics* (New York: Simon and Schuster, 1983), pages 38-39.

TEN—*A God Outside of Time, But Knowable*

1. Paul Kurtz, *Free Inquiry* (Winter 1992/93), pages 10-15.

2. John Maddox, "Down with the Big Bang," *Nature* 340 (1989), page 425.

3. Eric J. Lerner, *The Big Bang Never Happened* (New York: Random House, 1991); Eric J. Lerner, "The Big Bang Never Happened," *Discover* (June 1988), pages 70-79.

4. Jean-Claude Pecker, "Big Bangs, Plural: A Heretical View," *Free Inquiry* (Winter 1992/93), pages 10-11.

5. Milton Rothman, "What Went Before?" *Free Inquiry* (Winter 1992/93), page 12.

6. Victor J. Stenger, "The Face of Chaos," *Free Inquiry* (Winter 1992/93), page 14.

7. Adolf Grünbaum, "Pseudo-Creation of the 'Big Bang,'" *Free Inquiry* (Winter 1992/93), page 15.

8. Maddox, page 425.

9. Donald Lynden-Bell, J. Katz, and J. H. Redmount, "Sheet Universes and the Shapes of Friedmann Universes," *Monthly Notices of the Royal Astronomical Society* 239 (1989), page 201.

10. Hugh Ross, *The Fingerprint of God*, 2nd ed. rev. (Orange, CA: Promise Publishing, 1991), pages 89-94; Rosie Wyse, "Oldest Stars Are Older Still," *Nature* 361 (1993), pages 204-205.

11. Rothman, page 12.

12. Augustine of Hippo, "Confessions, Book Eleven, Chapters 10-14," *The Fathers of the Church*, vol. 21, *Confessions*, trans. Vernon J. Bourke (New York: Fathers of the Church, Inc., 1953), pages 339-344.

13. Fred Hoyle, *Quarterly Journal of the Royal Astronomical Society* 1 (1960), pages 28-39; Robert Jastrow and A. G. W. Cameron, ed., *Origin of the Solar System* (New York: Academic Press, 1963).

14. Lerner, *The Big Bang Never Happened*, pages 23-25.

ELEVEN—*A Brief Look at* A Brief History of Time

1. Stephen W. Hawking, *A Brief History of Time: From the Big Bang to Black Holes* (New York: Bantam Books, 1988), page 171.

2. Bryan Appleyard, "A Master of the Universe," *Sunday Times Magazine* (London), 19 July 1988, page 29.

3. Carl Sagan, "Introduction," *A Brief History of Time: From the Big Bang to Black Holes* (New York: Bantam Books, 1988), page x.

4. John Boslough, "Inside the Mind of a Genius," *Reader's Digest* (February 1984), page 120.

5. James B. Hartle and Steven W. Hawking, "Wave Function of the Universe," *Physical Review D* 28 (1983), pages 2960-2975.
6. Leon Jaroff, "Roaming the Cosmos," *Time*, 8 February 1988, page 60; Hawking, page 136, 141.
7. Hawking, page 136.
8. Heinz R. Pagels, *Perfect Symmetry: The Search for the Beginning of Time* (New York: Simon & Schuster, 1985), page 243.
9. Frank Tipler, "The Mind of God," *The Times Higher Education Supplement* (London), 14 October 1988, page 23.
10. Hawking, page 139.
11. 2 Timothy 1:9 and Titus 1:2. See also table 10.1, page 78.
12. Hawking, page 122.
13. Hawking, page 140.
14. Hawking, page 13.
15. Hawking, page 12.
16. Hawking, page 166.
17. Hawking, page 169.
18. Hawking, page 175.
19. Stanley L. Jaki, *Cosmos and Creator* (Edinburgh, U.K.: Scottish Academic Press, 1980), pages 49-54; Stanley L. Jaki, *God and the Cosmologists* (Washington, DC: Regnery Gateway, 1989), pages 104-109.
20. Hawking, page 168.
21. Hawking, page 126.
22. Hawking, page 168.
23. Hugh Ross, *The Fingerprint of God*, 2nd ed. rev. (Orange, CA: Promise, 1991), pages 124-128.
24. Hawking, page 174.

TWELVE—A Modern-Day Goliath

1. Allen Emerson, "A Disorienting View of God's Creation," *Christianity Today*, 1 February 1985, page 19.
2. Paul Davies, *God and the New Physics* (New York: Simon and Schuster, 1983), pages 25-43, specifically pages 38-39.
3. Davies, *God and the New Physics*, pages 167-174.
4. Paul Davies, *Superforce: The Search for a Grand Unified Theory of Nature* (New York: Simon and Schuster, 1984), page 243.
5. Paul Davies, *The Cosmic Blueprint: New Discoveries in Nature's Creative Ability to Order the Universe* (New York: Simon and Schuster, 1988), page 141.
6. Davies, *The Cosmic Blueprint*, page 203.
7. Richard J. Gott III, "Creation of Open Universes from de Sitter Space," *Nature* 295 (1982), page 304-307.
8. Gott, page 306.
9. Gott, page 306.
10. Davies, *God and the New Physics*, pages 172-174. Recently, while writing a science fiction novel, Carl Sagan asked his friend Kip Thorne, one of the world's experts on black holes, to calculate if there was any possibility for time travel from one universe to any other possibly existing one. Thorne's answer was that tunnels conceivably could exist between one universe and another but that the tunnels would be so small that nothing, not even the tiniest quantum entities, could possibly travel through them.
11. Heinz R. Pagels, "Uncertainty and Complementarity," *The World Treasury of Physics, Astronomy, and Mathematics*, ed. Timothy Ferris (Boston, MA: Little, Brown and Co., 1991), pages 106-108.
12. Nick Herbert, *Quantum Reality: Beyond the New Physics: An Excursion into Metaphysics and the Meaning of Reality* (New York: Anchor Books, Doubleday, 1987), pages 16-29; Stanley L. Jaki, *Cosmos and Creator* (Edinburgh, U.K.: Scottish Academic Press, 1980), pages 96-98; James Jeans, "A Universe of Pure Thought," *Quantum Questions*, ed.

Ken Wilber (Boston, MA: New Science Library, Shambhala, 1985), pages 140-144; Ken Wilber, *Quantum Questions* (Boston, MA: New Science Library, Shambhala, 1985), pages 145-146; Paul Teller, "Relativity, Relational Holism, and the Bell Inequalities," *Philosophical Consequences of Quantum Theory: Reflections on Bell's Theorem*, ed. James T. Cushing and Eman McMullin (Notre Dame, IN: University of Notre Dame Press, 1989), pages 216-223.

13. James S. Trefil, *The Moment of Creation* (New York: Charles Scribner's Sons, 1983), pages 91-101.

14. David Dvorkin, "Why I Am Not a Jew," *Free Inquiry* 10, no. 2 (1990), page 34. David Dvorkin points out that orthodox Jews and fundamentalist Christians share many beliefs in common and also share the tendency to add dogmas to their doctrines.

THIRTEEN—*The Divine Watchmaker*

1. William Paley, *Natural Theology on Evidence and Attributes of Deity*, 18th ed. rev. (Edinburgh, U.K.: Lackington, Allen and Co., and James Sawers, 1818), pages 12-14.

2. David Hume, *Dialogues Concerning Natural Religion*, Fontana Library Edition (London: Collins, 1963), pages 154-156.

3. Jacques Monod, *Chance and Necessity* (London: Collins, 1972), page 110 (emphasis in original).

4. Richard Dawkins, *The Blind Watchmaker: Why the Evidence of Evolution Reveals a Universe Without Design* (New York: W. W. Norton, 1987), page 5 (emphasis in original).

5. Stephen Jay Gould, *The Panda's Thumb: More Reflections in Natural History* (New York: W. W. Norton, 1980).

6. J. Raloff, "Earth Day 1980: The 29th Day?" *Science News* 117 (1980), page 270; Roger Lewin, "No Dinosaurs This Time," *Science* 221 (1983), page 1169.

7. Paul R. Ehrlich, Anne H. Ehrlich, and J. P. Holdren, *Ecoscience: Population, Resources, Environment* (San Francisco, CA: W. H. Freeman, 1977), page 142; Paul R. Ehrlich and Anne H. Ehrlich, *Extinction: The Causes and Consequences of the Disappearance of Species* (New York: Ballantine, 1981), page 33.

8. Ehrlich and Ehrlich, page 23.

9. Peter Gordon, "The Panda's Thumb Revisited: An Analysis of Two Arguments Against Design," *Origins Research* 7, no. 1 (1984), pages 12-14.

FOURTEEN—*A "Just Right" Universe*

1. Richard Swinburne, "Argument from the Fine-Tuning of the Universe," *Physical Cosmology and Philosophy*, ed. John Leslie (New York: Macmillan, 1991), page 160; Hugh Ross, *The Fingerprint of God*, 2nd ed. rev. (Orange, CA: Promise, 1991), page 122.

2. Ross, pages 122-123.

3. Fred Hoyle, *Galaxies, Nuclei, and Quasars* (New York: Harper and Row, 1965), pages 147-150; Fred Hoyle, "The Universe: Past and Present Reflection," *Annual Reviews of Astronomy and Astrophysics* 20 (1982), page 16; Ross, pages 126-127.

4. Fred Hoyle, *The Nature of the Universe*, 2nd ed. rev. (Oxford, U.K.: Basil Blackwell, 1952), page 109; Fred Hoyle, *Astronomy and Cosmology: A Modern Course* (San Francisco, CA: W. H. Freeman, 1975), pages 684-685; Hoyle, "The Universe: Past and Present Reflection," page 3; Hoyle, *Astronomy and Cosmology*, page 522.

5. Hoyle, *The Nature of the Universe*, page 111.

6. Hoyle, "The Universe: Past and Present Reflection," page 16.

7. John D. Barrow and Frank J. Tipler, *The Anthropic Cosmological Principle* (New York: Oxford University Press, 1986), page 400.

8. James S. Trefil, *The Moment of Creation* (New York: Collier Books, Macmillan, 1983), pages 127-134.

9. George F.R. Ellis, "The Anthropic Principle: Laws and Environments," in *The Anthropic Principle*, F. Bertola and U. Curi, ed. (New York: Cambridge University Press, 1993), page 30; D. Allan Bromley, "Physics: Atomic and Molecular Physics," *Science* 209 (1980), page 116.

10. George F.R. Ellis, page 30; H.R. Marston, S.H. Allen, and S.L. Swaby, "Iron Metabolism in Copper-Deficient Rats," *British Journal of Nutrition* 25 (1971), pages 15-30;

K.W.J. Wahle and N.T. Davies, "Effect of Dietary Copper Deficiency in the Rat on Fatty Acid Compostion of Adipose Tissue and Desaturase Activity of Liver Microsomes," *British Journal of Nutrition* 34 (1975), pages 105-112; Walter Mertz, "The Newer Essential Trace Elements, Chromium, Tin, Vanadium, Nickel, and Silicon," *Proceedings of the Nutrition Society*, 33 (1974), pages 307-313.

11. John P. Cox and R. Thomas Giuli, *Principles of Stellar Structure, Volume II: Applications to Stars* (New York: Gordon and Breach, 1968), pages 944-1028.

12. Ross, pages 120-128; Barrow and Tipler, pages 123-457; Bernard J. Carr and Martin J. Rees, "The Anthropic Principle and the Structure of the Physical World," *Nature* 278 (1979), pages 605-612; John M. Templeton, "God Reveals Himself in the Astronomical and in the Infinitesimal," *Journal of the American Scientific Affiliation* (December 1984), pages 194-200; Jim W. Neidhardt, "The Anthropic Principle: A Religious Response," *Journal of the American Scientific Affiliation* (December 1984), pages 201-207; Brandon Carter, "Large Number Coincidences and the Anthropic Principle in Cosmology," *Proceedings of the International Astronomical Union Symposium No. 63: Confrontation of Cosmological Theories with Observational Data*, ed. M. S. Longair (Boston, MA: Reidel Publishing, 1974), pages 291-298; John D. Barrow, "The Lore of Large Numbers: Some Historical Background to the Anthropic Principle," *Quarterly Journal of the Royal Astronomical Society* 22 (1981), pages 404-420; Alan Lightman, "To the Dizzy Edge," *Science* 82 (October 1982), pages 24-25; Thomas O'Toole, "Will the Universe Die by Fire or Ice?" *Science* 81 (April 1981), pages 71-72; Hoyle, *Galaxies, Nuclei, and Quasars*, pages 147-150; Bernard J. Carr, "On the Origin, Evolution, and Purpose of the Physical Universe," *Physical Cosmology and Philosophy*, ed. John Leslie (New York: Macmillan, 1990), pages 134-153; Swinburne, pages 154-173; R. E. Davies and R. H. Koch, "All the Observed Universe Has Contributed to Life," *Philosophical Transactions of the Royal Society of London*, series B, 334 (1991), pages 391-403; George F.R. Ellis, pages 27-32; Hubert Reeves, "Growth of Complexity in an Expanding Universe," in *The Anthropic Principle*, ed. F. Bertola and U. Curi (New York: Cambridge University Press, 1993), pages 67-84.

13. Davies and Koch, pages 391-403. See also chapters 3 and 4.

14. Hoyle, "The Universe," page 16.

15. Paul Davies, *God and the New Physics* (New York: Simon & Schuster, 1983), pages viii, 3-42, 142-143.

16. Paul Davies, *Superforce* (New York: Simon & Schuster, 1984), page 243.

17. Paul Davies, *The Cosmic Blueprint* (New York: Simon & Schuster, 1988), page 203; Paul Davies, "The Anthropic Principle," *Science Digest* 191, no. 10 (October 1983), page 24.

18. George Greenstein, *The Symbiotic Universe* (New York: William Morrow, 1988), page 27.

19. Tony Rothman, "A 'What You See Is What You Beget' Theory," *Discover* (May 1987), page 99.

20. Carr and Rees, page 612.

21. Carr, page 153 (emphasis in the original).

22. Freeman Dyson, *Infinite in All Directions* (New York: Harper and Row, 1988), page 298.

23. Henry Margenau and Roy Abraham Varghese, ed., *Cosmos, Bios, and Theos* (La Salle, IL: Open Court, 1992), page 52.

24. Margenau and Varghese, ed., page 83.

25. Stuart Gannes, *Fortune*, 13 October 1986, page 57.

26. Fang Li Zhi and Li Shu Xian, *Creation of the Universe*, trans. T. Kiang (Singapore: World Scientific, 1989), page 173.

27. Roger Penrose, in the movie *A Brief History of Time* (Burbank, CA: Paramount Pictures Incorporated, 1992).

28. George F.R.Ellis, page 30.

29. Edward Harrison, *Masks of the Universe* (New York: Collier Books, Macmillan, 1985), pages 252, 263.

30. John Noble Wilford, "Sizing Up the Cosmos: An Astronomer's Quest," *New York*

Times, 12 March 1991, page B9.
31. Tim Stafford, "Cease-fire in the Laboratory," *Christianity Today*, 3 April 1987, page 18.
32. Robert Jastrow, "The Secret of the Stars," *New York Times Magazine*, 25 June 1978, page 7.
33. Robert Jastrow, *God and the Astronomers* (New York: W. W. Norton, 1978), page 116.
34. Swinburne, page 165.
35. William Lane Craig, "Barrow and Tipler on the Anthropic Principle Versus Divine Design," *British Journal of Philosophy and Science* 38 (1988), page 392.
36. Joseph Silk, *Cosmic Enigma* (1993), pages 8-9.
37. NCSE staff, *Education and Creationism Don't Mix* (Berkeley, CA: National Center for Science Education, 1985), page 3; Eugenie C. Scott, "Of Pandas and People," *National Center for Science Education Reports* (January-February 1990), page 18; Paul Bartelt, "Patterson and Gish at Morningside College," *The Committees of Correspondence*, Iowa Committee of Correspondence Newsletter, vol. 4, no. 4 (October 1989), page 1.
38. *Education and Creationism Don't Mix*, page 3; Eugenie C. Scott and Henry P. Cole, "The Elusive Scientific Basis of Creation Science," *The Quarterly Review of Biology* (March 1985), page 297.
39. Ilya Prigogine and Isabelle Stengers, *Order Out Of Chaos: Man's New Dialogue With Nature* (New York: Bantam Books, 1984).
40. Barrow and Tipler.
41. Barrow and Tipler, page 676-677.
42. Barrow and Tipler, pages 676-677, 682; Martin Gardner, "Notes of a Fringe-Watcher: Tipler's Omega Point Theory," *Skeptical Inquirer* 15, no. 2 (1991), pages 128-132.
43. Frank J. Tipler, *The Physics of Immortality: Modern Cosmology, God, and the Resurrection of the Dead* (New York: Doubleday, 1994).
44. Martin Gardner, "WAP, SAP, PAP, and FAP," *The New York Review of Books*, vol. 23, no. 8, 8 May 1986, pages 22-25.
45. Roger Penrose, *The Emperor's New Mind* (New York: Oxford University Press, 1989), pages 3-145, 374-451; Roger Penrose, *Shadows of the Mind* (New York: Oxford University Press, 1994), pages 7-208.
46. Frank J. Tipler, pages 253-255.
47. Frank J. Tipler, pages 256-257.
48. Gardner, "Notes of a Fringe-Watcher," page 132.

FIFTEEN—Earth: The Place for Life

1. Iosef S. Shklovskii and Carl Sagan, *Intelligent Life in the Universe* (San Francisco, CA: Holden-Day, 1966), pages 343-350.
2. Shklovskii and Sagan, page 413.
3. Dava Sobel, "Is Anybody Out There?" *Life* (September 1992), page 62.
4. Ron Cowen, "Were Spiral Galaxies Once More Common," *Science News* 142 (1992), page 390; Alan Dressler, et al., "New Images of the Distant, Rich Cluster CL 0939+4713 with WFPC2," *Astrophysical Journal Letters* 435 (1994), pages L23-L26.
5. R. E. Davies and R. H. Koch, "All the Observed Universe Has Contributed to Life," *Philosophical Transactions of the Royal Society of London*, series B, 334 (1991), pages 391-403.
6. John Maddox, "The Anthropic View of Nucleosynthesis," *Nature* 355 (1992), page 107.
7. Robert H. Dicke, "Dirac's Cosmology and Mach's Principle," *Nature* 192 (1961), page 440.
8. Michael H. Hart, "Habitable Zones About Main Sequence Stars," *Icarus* 37 (1979), pages 351-357.
9. George Abell, *Exploration of the Universe* (New York: Holt, Rinehart, and Winston, 1964), pages 244-247; John C. Brandt and Paul W. Hodge, *Solar System Astrophysics* (New York: McGraw-Hill, 1964), pages 395-416.
10. Charles B. Thaxton, Walter L. Bradley, and Roger L. Olsen, *The Mystery of Life's Origin: Reassessing Current Theories* (New York: Philosophical Library, 1984), pages 43-46, 73-94.

11. Gregory S. Jenkins, Hall G. Marshall, and W.R. Kuhn, "Pre-Cambrian Climate: The Effects of Land Area and Earth's Rotation Rate," *Journal of Geophysical Research*, Series D, 98 (1993), pages 8785-8791; K.J. Zahnle and J.C.G. Walker, "A Constant Daylength During the Precambrian Era?" *Precambrian Research* 37 (1987), pages 95-105; R. Monastersky, "Speedy Spin Kept Early Earth From Freezing," *Science News* 143 (1993), page 373.

12. W.R. Kuhn, J.C.G. Walker, and H.G. Marshall, "The Effect on Earth's Surface Temperature from Variations in Rotation Rate, Continent Formation, Solar Luminosity, and Carbon Dioxide," *Journal of Geophysical Research* 94 (1989), pages 11, 129-11, 136; R. Monastersky, page 373.

13. The editors, "Our Friend Jove," *Discover* (July 1993), page 15.

14. Hugh Ross, "Dinosaurs' Disappearance No Longer a Mystery," *Facts & Faith*, vol. 5, no. 3 (1991), pages 1-3.

15. Mordecai-Mark Lac Low and Kevin Zahnle, "Explosion of Comet Shoemaker-Levy 9 on Entry into the Jovian Atmosphere," *Astrophysical Journal Letters* 434 (1994), pages L33-L36; Ron Cowen, "By Jupiter! Comet Crashes Dazzle and Delight," *Science News* 146 (1994), page 55.

16. The editors, page 15.

17. Jacques Laskar, "Large-Scale Chaos in the Solar System," *Astronomy and Astrophysics* 287 (1994), page 112.

18. William R. Ward, "Comments on the Long-Term Stability of the Earth's Obliquity," *Icarus* 50 (1982), pages 444-448; Carl D. Murray, "Seasoned Travellers," *Nature* 361 (1993), pages 586-587; Jacques Laskar and P. Robutel, "The Chaotic Obliquity of the Planets," *Nature* 361 (1993), pages 608-612; Jacques Laskar, F. Joutel, and P. Robutel, "Stabilization of the Earth's Obliquity by the Moon," *Nature* 361 (1993), pages 615-617.

19. H. E. Newsom and S. R. Taylor, "Geochemical Implications of the Formation of the Moon by a Single Giant Impact," *Nature* 338 (1989), pages 29-34; W. M. Kaula, "Venus: A Contrast in Evolution to Earth," *Science* 247 (1990), pages 1191-1196.

20. Davies and Koch, pages 391-403; Hart, pages 351-357; Ward, pages 444-448; Murray, pages 586-587; Laskar and Robutel, pages 608-612; Laskar, Joutel, and Robutel, pages 615-617; Newsom and Taylor, pages 29-34; Kaula, pages 1191-1196; Robert T. Rood and James S. Trefil, *Are We Alone? The Possibility of Extraterrestrial Civilizations* (New York: Scribner's Sons, 1983); John D. Barrow and Frank J. Tipler, *The Anthropic Cosmological Principle* (New York: Oxford University Press, 1986), pages 510-575; Don L. Anderson, "The Earth as a Planet: Paradigms and Paradoxes," *Science* 22, no. 3 (1984), pages 347-355; I. H. Campbell and S. R. Taylor, "No Water, No Granite—No Oceans, No Continents," *Geophysical Research Letters* 10 (1983), pages 1061-1064; Brandon Carter, "The Anthropic Principle and Its Implications for Biological Evolution," *Philosophical Transactions of the Royal Society of London*, series A, 310 (1983), pages 352-363; Allen H. Hammond, "The Uniqueness of the Earth's Climate," *Science* 187 (1975), page 245; Owen B. Toon and Steve Olson, "The Warm Earth," *Science* 85 (October 1985), pages 50-57; George Gale, "The Anthropic Principle," *Scientific American* 245, no. 6 (1981), pages 154-171; Hugh Ross, *Genesis One: A Scientific Perspective* (Pasadena, CA: Reasons To Believe, 1983), pages 6-7; Ron Cottrell, *The Remarkable Spaceship Earth* (Denver, CO: Accent Books, 1982); Ter D. Haar, "On the Origin of the Solar System," *Annual Review of Astronomy and Astrophysics* 5 (1967), pages 267-278; George Greenstein, *The Symbiotic Universe* (New York: William Morrow, 1988), pages 68-97; John M. Templeton, "God Reveals Himself in the Astronomical and in the Infinitesimal," *Journal of the American Scientific Affiliation* (December 1984), pages 196-198; Michael H. Hart, "The Evolution of the Atmosphere of the Earth," *Icarus* 33 (1978), pages 23-39; Tobias Owen, Robert D. Cess, and V. Ramanathan, "Enhanced CO_2 Greenhouse to Compensate for Reduced Solar Luminosity on Early Earth," *Nature* 277 (1979), pages 640-641; John Gribbin, "The Origin of Life: Earth's Lucky Break," *Science Digest* (May 1983), pages 36-102; P.J.E. Peebles and Joseph Silk, "A Cosmic Book of Phenomena," *Nature* 346 (1990), pages 233-239; Michael H. Hart, "Atmospheric Evolution, the Drake Equation, and DNA: Sparse Life in an Infinite

Universe," *Philosophical Cosmology and Philosophy*, ed. John Leslie (New York: Macmillan, 1990), pages 256-266; Stanley L. Jaki, *God and the Cosmologists* (Washington, DC: Regnery Gateway, 1989), pages 177-184; R. Monastersky, page 373; the editors, page 15; Jacques Laskar, pages 109-113; Richard A. Kerr, "The Solar System's New Diversity," *Science* 265 (1994), pages 1360-1362; Richard A. Kerr, "When Comparative Planetology Hit Its Target," *Science* 265 (1994), page 1361; W.R. Kuhn, J.C.G. Walker, and H.G. Marshall, pages 11,129-131,136; Gregory S. Jenkins, Hal G. Marshall and W.R. Kuhn, pages 8785-8791; K.J. Zahnle and J.C.G. Walker, pages 95-105; M.J. Newman and R.T. Roos, "Implications of the Solar Evolution for the Earth's Early Atmosphere," *Science* 198 (1977), pages 1035-1037; J.C.G. Walker and K.J. Zahnle, "Lunar Nodal Tides and Distance to the Moon During the Precambrian," *Nature* 320 (1986), pages 600-602; J.F. Kasting and J.B. Pollack, "Effects of High CO^2 Levels on Surface Temperatures and Atmospheric Oxidation State of the Early Earth," *Journal of Atmospheric Chemistry* 1 (1984), pages 403-428; H.G. Marshall, J.C.G. Walker, and W.R. Kuhn, "Long Term Climate Change and the Geochemical Cycle of Carbon," *Journal of Geophysical Research* 93 (1988), pages 791-801.

SIXTEEN—*Building Life*

1. Christopher Chyba and Carl Sagan, "Endogenous Production, Exogenous Delivery and Impact-shock Synthesis or Organic Molecules: An Inventory for the Origins of Life," *Nature* 355 (1992), pages 125-132.
2. Manfred Schidlowski, "A 3,800-million-year Isotopic Record of Life from Carbon in Sedimentary Rocks," *Nature* 333 (1988), pages 313-318.
3. Kevin A. Maher and David J. Stevenson, "Impact Frustration of the Origin of Life," *Nature* 331 (1988), pages 612-614; Verne R. Oberbeck and Guy Fogleman, "Impacts and the Origin of Life," *Nature* 339 (1989), page 434; Norman H. Sleep, et al., "Annihilation of Ecosystems by Large Asteroid Impacts on the Early Earth," *Nature* 342 (1989), pages 139-142.
4. Maher and Stevenson, pages 612-614.
5. Charles B. Thaxton, Walter L. Bradley, and Roger L. Olsen, *The Mystery of Life's Origin: Reassessing Current Theories* (New York: Philosophical Library, 1984), pages 69-98; Walter L. Bradley, private communication (1993).
6. Chyba and Sagan, page 128.
7. Gordon Schlesinger and Stanley L. Miller, "Prebiotic Synthesis in Atmospheres Containing CH, CO, and CO2," *Journal of Molecular Evolution* 19 (1983), pages 376-382.
8. Robert Shapiro, *Origins: A Skeptic's Guide to the Creation of Life on Earth* (New York: Summit Books, 1986), page 128.
9. Michael H. Hart, "Atmospheric Evolution, the Drake Equation, and DNA: Sparse Life in an Infinite Universe," *Physical Cosmology and Philosophy*, ed. John Leslie (New York: Macmillan, 1990), pages 263-264.
10. Hubert P. Yockey, "An Application of Information Theory to the Central Dogma and the Sequence Hypothesis," *Journal of Theoretical Biology* 46 (1974), pages 369-406; Hubert P. Yockey, "On the Information Content of Cytochrome c," *Journal of Theoretical Biology* 67 (1977), pages 345-376; Hubert P. Yockey, "A Calculation of the Probability of Spontaneous Biogenesis by Information Theory," *Journal of Theoretical Biology* 67 (1977), pages 377-398; Hubert P. Yockey, "Do Overlapping Genes Violate Molecular Biology and the Theory of Evolution?" *Journal of Theoretical Biology* 80 (1979), pages 21-26; Hubert P. Yockey, "Self Organization Origin of Life Scenarios and Information Theory," *Journal of Theoretical Biology* 91 (1981), pages 13-31.
11. Hubert P. Yockey, *Information Theory and Molecular Biology* (Cambridge, U.K.: Cambridge University Press, 1992), pages 231-309.
12. M. Mitchell Waldrop, "Finding RNA Makes Proteins Gives 'RNA World' a Big Boost," *Science* 256 (1992), pages 1396-1397.
13. Thomas R. Cech, "The Chemistry of Self-Splicing RNA and RNA Enzymes," *Science* 236 (1987), pages 1532-1539.
14. Harry F. Noller, Veronita Hoffarth, and Ludwika Zimniak, "Unusual Resistance of Peptidyl Transferase to Protein Extraction Procedures," *Science* 256 (1992), pages

1416-1419.
15. Joseph A. Piccirilli, et al., "Aminoacyl Esterase Activity of the Tetrahymena Ribozyme," *Science* 256 (1992), pages 1420-1424.
16. John Horgan, "In the Beginning," *Scientific American* (February 1991), page 119.
17. Robert Shapiro, "Prebiotic Ribose Synthesis: A Critical Analysis," *Origin of Life and Evolution of the Biosphere* 18 (1988), pages 71-85.
18. Horgan, page 119; Robert Shapiro, "Protometabolism: A Scenario for the Origin of Life," *The American Scientist* (July-August 1992), page 387.
19. Fred Hoyle and Chandra Wickramasinghe, *Evolution from Space* (New York: Simon and Schuster, 1981), pages 39-61; Iosef S. Shklovskii and Carl Sagan, *Intelligent Life in the Universe* (San Francisco, CA: Holden-Day, 1966), pages 207-211; the item on meteorites came from a report of a computer analysis that was presented at the Twentieth Lunar and Planetary Science Conference (1989), Houston, Texas.
20. Shapiro, *Origins*.
21. Yockey, *Information Theory and Molecular Biology*.
22. Charles B. Thaxton, Walter L. Bradley, and Roger L. Olsen, *The Mystery of Life's Origin: Reassessing Current Theories* (New York: Philosophical Library, 1984).
23. Romans 10:18, *New King James Version*.

SEVENTEEN—Extra-Dimensional Power

1. Jeremy Bernstein, *The Tenth Dimension: An Informal History of High Energy Physics* (New York: McGraw-Hill, 1989), pages 152-153.
2. Hugh Ross, *Above and Beyond Us* (Pasadena, CA: Reasons To Believe, 1993). This one-hour video documentary was aired on the Trinity Broadcasting Network and is now being distributed on VHS cassettes.
3. Genesis 16:13, 28:16; Deuteronomy 30:14; Psalm 34:18, 119:151, 145:18; Jeremiah 23:24; Acts 17:28; and Romans 10:8 are a few of many examples.
4. Genesis 28:16; Exodus 33:20; Job 9:11, 37:23; and John 6:46 are a few of many examples.
5. 1 Timothy 6:16.
6. Edwin Abbott, *Flatland: A Romance of Many Dimensions*, with notes by David W. Davies (Pasadena, CA: Grant Daehlstrom, 1978).
7. Ross, *Above and Beyond Us*.
8. John 16:5-10.
9. John 16:6.
10. John 16:7.
11. Philippians 2:5-9.
12. John 14:12-14.
13. Matthew 28:20.

EIGHTEEN—The Point

1. Hebrews 11:6.
2. Psalm 34:18, 145:18.
3. Ephesians 2:13.
4. J.N.D. Anderson, *The Evidence for the Resurrection* (Downers Grove, IL: InterVarsity Press, 1966).
5. James 4:8.
6. Revelation 3:8.

NAME INDEX

Abbott, Edwin, 159
Alfvén, Hans, 84
Aristotle, 122
Arp, Halton, 83
Augustine, 84

Barrow, John, 128-129
Bludman, Sidney, 67
Bohr, Niels, 100-101
Bondi, Herman, 59-60
Bradley, Walter, 156
Burbidge, Geoffrey, 20, 25, 77, 80
Burnham, Frederic, 19

Carr, Bernard, 122
Cheng, Edward, 25
Christ Jesus, 78-80, 95, 156, 160-161, 163-164
Chyba, Christopher, 147-149
Copernicus, Nicolas, 57
Craig, William Lane, 126

Darwin, Charles, 106-108
David, King, 164
Davies, Paul, 95-98, 121
Davies, R.E., 132-133
Dawkins, Richard, 107
Dicke, Robert, 64, 133
Drake, Frank, 131
Duncan, Douglas, 40
Dyson, Freeman, 122

Eddington, Arthur, 57, 73
Ehrlich, Anne, 109

Ehrlich, Paul, 109
Einstein, Albert, 40-41, 49, 51-55, 57, 73, 75-76, 100, 122
Ellis, George, 73, 76, 123

Fang Li Zhi, 123
Frenk, Carlos, 19

Gamow, George, 20-22
Gardner, Martin, 129
Gödel, Kurt, 91
Gold, Thomas, 59
Gordon, Peter, 110
Gott III, Richard, 98-99
Gould, Stephen, 106-107, 110
Greenstein, George, 121
Gribbin, John, 61-62, 64
Griffiths, Robert, 124
Grünbaum, Adolf, 82, 84
Guth, Alan, 66-67, 98

Hamilton, Donald, 45, 60
Hari, Mata, 130
Harrison, Edward, 123-124
Hart, Michael, 151
Hartle, James, 89
Hawking, Jane, 88
Hawking, Stephen, 19, 54, 73, 76, 87-92, 95
Hitler, Adolf, 130
Hoyle, Fred, 59-60, 113, 121
Hubbard, L. Ron, 130
Hubble, Edwin, 52-53, 55, 58
Hume, David, 106-108, 127

Israel, Werner, 67

Jastrow, Robert, 124
Jeans, James, 60
Job, 91

Kant, Immanuel, 49-51
Katz, J., 82
Kistiakowsky, Vera, 122
Koch, R.H., 132-133
Koppel, Ted, 19, 154

Lambert, David, 40
Laskar, Jacques, 133
Lemke, Michael, 40
Lerner, Eric, 71-72, 84-85
Linde, André, 67
Linsky, Jeffrey, 37
Li Shu Xian, 123
Lynden-Bell, Donald, 82

Maddox, John, 81-83, 133
Mather, John, 24
Meyer, David, 28
Monod, Jacques, 107
Morowitz, Harold, 149-151

Newton, Isaac, 38, 49, 51
Novikov, Igor, 67

Olsen, Roger, 156
Orgel, Leslie, 153

Page, Don, 88
Pagels, Heinz, 89
Paley, William, 105-108, 110, 123
Paul, 93, 156, 159
Pecker, Jean-Claude, 82-83
Penrose, Roger, 73, 74, 75-76, 123, 129

Penzias, Arno, 22, 122
Polyakov, Alexander, 123
Prigogine, Ilya, 127-128
Proxmire, William, 145

Redmount, J.H., 82
Rees, Martin, 122
Roche, George, 9
Rothman, Milton, 82-83
Rothman, Tony, 122

Sagan, Carl, 88, 131, 134, 147-149
Sandage, Allan, 123-124
Shapiro, Robert, 153, 156
Sher, Marc, 66-67
Shklovskii, Iosef, 131, 134
Sikkema, Arnold, 67
Silk, Joseph, 126
Smoot, George, 19, 33
Steidel, Charles, 45
Stenger, Victor, 82, 84
Swinburne, Richard, 126

Thaxton, Charles, 156
Tifft, William, 83
Tipler, Frank, 90, 128-130
Tolman, Richard, 20
Turner, Michael, 19, 33

Vilenkin, Alexander, 75

Wetherill, George, 137
Wilson, Robert, 22

Yockey, Hubert, 152, 156

Zel'dovich, Yakob, 67

SUBJECT INDEX

Absolute zero, 22, 27
Abundances of elements, 22, 24, 28
Adiabatic expansion, 75
Age of the universe, 22, 43, 49,
 58-61, 117, 119, 150
Agnosticism, 103, 123
Albedo, 140, 142-143
Alternate life forms, 133
Amino acids, 133, 151-153
Ammonia, 135-136, 140
Anomalous redshifts, 83
Anthropic principle, 92, 121-125, 128
Anthropomorphism, 126
Anti-nucleons, 114, 120
Apparent design, 106-107
Association of Women in Science, 122
Asteroids, 32, 51, 140, 144
Astrophysical Research Consortium,
 46
Atheism, 77, 81-85, 89-90, 121, 124,
 127
Atmosphere, 135-136, 140-144, 149
Atomic nuclei, 112, 114, 118
Axial tilt, 140, 143

Bachelor stars, 134, 139, 144
"Bad designs," 107, 110
Beginner, 14, 52, 63, 89
Beginning, 14, 22-23, 52, 57, 60, 62-64,
 71, 73, 75-78, 80-81, 84, 88-90, 96,
 102
Beryllium abundance, 38-40, 41, 43,
 46, 113, 120
Bible, 15-17, 54, 57-58, 61, 76-81, 84,
 87-88, 91-93, 95-96, 103, 109, 130,
 157, 159, 163-165
Big bang, 14, 19-20, 24, 26-28, 31, 33,
 38, 60-63, 71-73, 75-76, 80-85, 114,
 118, 126, 158
Big bang ripples, 33, 35, 44
Binaries, white dwarf, 121, 133, 139,
 143

Binary pulsars, 74-75
Binary stars, 51, 133
Biosphere, 135
Black holes, 68, 74, 87, 114, 119-120
Blind watchmaker, 107, 123
Boron abundance, 38-40, 41, 43, 46,
 119, 133
Bounce mechanism, 63-68, 72
Brown dwarfs, 38
Buddhism, 69
Building blocks, 49, 111, 149-150

Carbon, 28, 113, 120, 133, 147-148
Carbon dioxide, 141, 144
Causality, 76, 78, 84, 100, 102
Cause and effect, 52, 75-78, 80, 82, 84,
 88, 95-96, 100, 102, 127
Cepheid variables, 42
Chaos, 123, 127
Christian Science, 79
Classical physics, 90, 102
Climatic runaways, 120, 135, 138,
 140-141
Cold dark matter, 32, 46
Comets, 51, 137, 140, 144, 148
Consciousness, 129-130
Copenhagen interpretation, 100-101
Copper, 116
Cosmic Background Explorer
 Satellite (COBE), 19-26, 40-41, 46,
 85
Cosmic background radiation, 22-28,
 32-33, 44-46, 85, 122
Council for Democratic and Secular
 Humanism, 81
Craters, 148, 155
Creation days, 58, 61, 109-110
Creation events, 15, 61
Creationists, 58, 82
Creation, transcendent, 76-79, 130,
 157
Critical mass, 37, 63, 66

Crustal thickness, 140, 143
Dark matter, 32-38, 44
Dark night sky paradox, 50-51
Darwinism, 49, 106-110, 125, 135. *See also* Evolutionism
Deceleration of the universe, 43, 52
Deism, 20, 90-91, 123
Dependency factors, 142-144
Deuterium abundance, 28, 36-40, 43-46, 119, 125
Differential microwave radiometers, 26-27
Diffuse hot intergalactic gas, 43-44
DNA, 120, 149, 151-153
Dog breeding, 108
Domain, 67
Dust clouds, 50
Dwarf galaxies, 134

Earth, 15, 36, 40, 42, 50, 57, 71, 74, 78, 103, 106-108, 110, 117, 131-138, 141, 147-149, 154-155, 164
Earthquakes, 137, 141, 144
Echo-delay experiment, 73
Einstein's repulsive force, 52-54
Electromagnetism, 84-85, 91, 112, 115-119, 140
Electrons, 31, 74, 99, 112, 115, 118
Electron-to-proton mass ratio, 112, 119
Elements, abundances of, 22, 24
Elliptical galaxies, 132, 138
Enlightenment, 14
Entropy, 24, 65-66, 68, 71, 117, 128
Enzymes, 152
Escape velocity, 135-136, 140, 143
Eternal life, 78
Evil, 130
Evolutionism, 57-58, 154-156. *See also* Darwinism.
Evolution reversal, 109-110
Exotic matter, 26, 31-33, 34-41, 43-46, 64, 85, 121
Expansion, adiabatic, 75
Expansion of the universe, 42-46, 52, 53, 58-65, 66, 83, 116, 119
Extinctions, 109-110, 132, 141
Extra dimensions, 16, 76-80, 88-89, 96, 97, 157-161

Extraterrestrial bombardments, 148
Extraterrestrial intelligent life, 131, 145

Final anthropic principle (FAP), 129
Fine structure constant, 119-120
First Church of Christ of the Big Bang, 20, 77
Flat-Earth Society, 103
Fluorine, 121, 133, 139
Fossil record, 109-110, 147
Free choice, 54-55, 77, 91, 157, 160
Free Inquiry, 81-82
Free-thinkers, 103
Freeways, 42
Fundamental particles, 31, 114
Fusion, nuclear, 22, 36, 113, 117-120, 125
Fuzzy logic, 127

Galaxies, 13, 20, 24-28, 32, 35, 37, 41-46, 51, 52-54, 59-61, 83-85, 92, 114-115, 117-121, 131-132, 143
  clumping of, 33, 38, 45-46, 84, 116
  clusters of, 24, 29, 32, 35, 41-42, 44, 46, 82, 84-85
  dwarf, 134
  elliptical, 132, 138
  formation of, 24-28, 31, 33, 35, 45, 59-60, 115, 119
  irregular, 132, 134, 138
  spiral, 132-133
Game theory, 130
Gas clouds, 28
General relativity, 10-11, 40, 49, 51-52, 73-75, 77, 80-82, 85, 89-90, 102, 158
Genes, 151
Genesis, 15, 58. *See also* Bible
Geography, 15
Geophysics, 15
Gideons, 15, 16
Globular clusters, 133
Glycine, 149
God of the gaps, 72
Grand unified theories, 97
Gravitational lensing, 38, 40-46
Gravity, 32, 40, 43, 54, 57, 63-64, 68,

73-74, 75, 84-85, 87, 91, 112-113, 115-118, 133, 155
surface, 135-136, 137, 140, 143
Gravity wave detector, 118
Greenhouse effect, 135, 138-140, 142, 144

Heaven, 130
Heavy elements, 20, 22, 112-114, 117-120, 125, 132-134, 138-139, 144
Heisenberg uncertainty principle, 92, 96
Helium, 20, 28, 113, 118-119, 125, 132
Hell, 130
Hemoglobin, 112
Hinduism, 63, 69, 100
Holy books, 15, 17, 77, 79
Holy Grail, 19, 33
Homogeneity of the universe, 92
Hot big bang, 19-20, 23-24, 27-29, 35, 46-47, 114
Hot dark matter, 32
Hubble Space Telescope, 36-42, 46
Hubble time, 58, 62-63, 71
Humanists, 102
Hurricanes, 136
Hydrocarbons, 141
Hydrogen, 20, 36, 112, 118, 125, 149
Hydrogen maser clock, 73

Imaginary time, 90
Incompleteness theorem, 91
Infinite universe, 49-50, 57, 61, 63, 71, 106
Inflationary big bang, 75, 98, 116
Information, 71, 98-99, 128, 153, 156
International Society for the Study of the Origin of Life, 153
Interstellar medium, 50, 132-134, 148
Invariance, principle of, 51-52
Irregular galaxies, 132, 134, 138
Islam, 79, 157

Jehovah's Witnesses, 79, 158
Judaism, 79
Jupiter, 50, 136, 137-138, 144, 155. *See also* Planets
Jurassic Park, 127

Keck Telescope, 27-28, 37, 45-46

Large Megellanic Cloud, 37, 44
Large-scale structure, 67
Laws of mechanics, 49, 51
Laws of physics, 68, 71-72, 89-91, 98, 99, 117, 121, 129
Lensing, gravitational, 40-46
Life chemistry, 22, 108, 110, 112-113, 117-119, 132, 134-135, 138-139, 148-149, 153-154
Life, extraterrestrial, 131, 145
Life forms, alternate, 133
Light pressure, 46
Light, velocity of, 32, 51-52, 119
Little bangs, 28
Longevity requirements, 142, 144

MACHOs, 37-38, 46
Macro-evolution, 109
Magnetic fields, 85, 140-141, 143
Mars, 148, 154-155. *See also* Planets
Mass density of the universe, 38, 43, 63-64, 66, 92, 119, 125
Materialism, 10, 58, 107, 109-110, 127, 135
Mechanical efficiency, 66
Mechanics
    laws of, 49, 51
    quantum, 68, 89, 92, 95-97, 99-102
    statistical, 108
Mercury, 134, 138, 148, 155. *See also* Planets
Mesons, 114
Metaphysics, 68, 123
Meteorites, 148, 155
Methane, 135-136, 140
Microevolution, 108
Micro-organisms, 154-155
Milky Way, 26, 132
Miracles, 127, 161
Missing mass, 36, 65
Molecular bonding, 112, 119
Moon, 73, 115, 131, 138, 141, 144, 148, 164
Morality, 10
Mormonism, 79
Mt. Wilson 100-inch telescope, 55
Multiple universes, 98-99, 123-126

Mutations, 106-108, 110

NASA, 40, 43, 73-74
National Center for Science
    Education, 127
Natural selection, 106-107
Nebulae, 50
Neutral atmosphere, 149
Neutron decay, 114, 120
Neutrons, 20, 22, 31, 36, 68, 112,
    114-115, 119, 125
Neutron stars, 75, 114, 120
New Age, 69, 87, 89, 95
New Testament, 16, 79, 92, 128, 160.
    See also Bible
Nitrogen, 113, 141, 144
No-God of the gaps, 72, 99
Non-theism, 72, 85, 98-99, 103, 111,
    125, 151-152
Nothing, 97
Nuclear force
    strong, 68, 91, 112-113, 116, 118
    weak, 91, 112-113, 116, 118
Nuclear fusion, 22, 28, 36, 113,
    117-120, 125
Nuclear ground state energies,
    112-113, 120
Nucleic acids, 150-151, 153-154
Nucleons, 22, 114-115
Nucleotides, 149-151, 153

Obliquity, 138, 141
Observer-created reality, 99-101
Ockham's razor, 97-98
Old Testament, 79. *See also* Bible
Omega Point, 129
Omega Point Theology (OPT), 130
Orbital eccentricity, 140, 143
Orbital inclination, 140-141, 143
Orbits, planetary, 120-121, 133-134,
    139
Ordinary matter, 25, 31-33, 36-38, 40,
    43-46, 121
Oscillating universe, 63-69, 71-72
Oxidizing atmosphere, 149
Oxygen, 113, 116, 120, 139-141, 144,
    149
Ozone, 140, 144

Paleontologists, 58, 106, 110
Panda's thumb, 107, 110
Pantheism, 76
Participatory anthropic principle
    (PAP), 129
Particle physics, 31, 68, 97, 102, 158
Particles, fundamental, 31
Particles, virtual, 96
Peptide bond, 152
Perfect radiator, 22-24, 26-29
Personality, 10, 55, 77, 124, 144-145,
    157
Phosphorus, 113
Photosynthesis, 139-140
Physics, laws of, 68, 71-72, 89-91, 98,
    99, 117, 121
Planetary, ages, 136, 139
Planetary, distances, 131, 134, 139,
    142-143
Planetary, formation, 119, 142
Planetary, orbits, 120-121, 133-134,
    139
Planets, 24, 33, 51, 84, 113-117,
    120-121, 125, 131-139, 142-144,
    154, 164
Plasma model, 81, 84-85
Prebiotic molecules, 148-149, 153
Prebiotic soups, 148-149, 152-153
Predestination, 54-55, 77
Predetermination, 91, 157, 160
Primeval radiation field, 98-99
Principle of invariance, 51-52
Proteins, 149-150, 152-154
Proto-galaxies, 119
Proton decay, 114-115, 120
Protons, 20, 22, 31-32, 36, 68, 74, 112,
    114-115, 119-120, 125
Proto-planets, 121, 139
Pulsars, 74-75

Quantum entities, 99, 101
Quantum events, 97, 99-100, 101, 102
Quantum gravity, 67-68, 85
Quantum mechanics, 68, 89, 92,
    95-97, 99-102
Quantum tunneling, 95-98, 116
Quasars, 41, 45-46, 83, 85

Radiation
  cosmic background, 22-28, 32-33, 43-45, 85, 122
  ultraviolet, 139-141, 155
Radiator, 22-24, 26-29
Radioactive decay, 113
Radiometers, differential microwave, 26-27
Random chance, 49, 123-124, 148, 150-151
Reasons To Believe, 17
Red dwarfs, 38
Redshifts, 45, 83
Reducing atmosphere, 149
Reincarnation, 63, 69
Relativity
  general, 10-11, 40, 49, 52, 54, 73-75, 77, 80-82, 85, 89-90, 102, 158
  special, 52, 116
Religion, 10, 15, 122. *See also individual religions by name*
Religious Science, 79
Revelation, 11
RNA, 149, 152-153
Roentgen Satellite (ROSAT), 43-44, 46
Rotation period, 134, 136-142
Roulette wheels, 99
Runaway boiling, 135, 138-140
Runaway freeze-up, 120, 135, 140

Salvation, 15, 95
Satellites, 50-51
  COBE, 19-29, 38-41, 45-46, 84-85
  ROSAT, 43-46
Saturn, 137-138, 144, 155. *See also* Planets
Scientology, 130
Second law of thermodynamics, 128
Seismic activity, 135-136, 141-142, 143-144
Self-organization, 82-84, 127-128
Sexual bliss, 130
Silicon, 133
Sin, 78-79
Singularity, 61-64, 81-82, 88-91
Solar system, 37, 83-85, 125-127, 132-133, 135-137, 144-145, 147, 154-155
Solar wind, 155

Space curvature, 68
Space-time theorem, 73, 75-76, 77, 79-80, 81-82, 88-90, 91-92
Special relativity, 52
Speciation, 108-109, 139-140, 143-144
Specific entropy, 23-24
Spiral galaxies, 132-133
Spontaneous self-generation, 81-84, 152, 153-154
Standard big bang, 75-76
Star birth date, 134, 139-140, 143-144
Star burning, 60, 82-83, 112-113, 117-119, 125, 134-135, 139-140
Star clusters, 50-51, 81-82, 83-84, 119, 133
Star formation, 114-117, 118-121, 132, 138-139, 141-142
Starlight, 40-41, 49-50, 73
Stars, 13-14, 23-24, 28, 38-41, 44, 49-51, 60, 81-83, 112-121, 125, 131-132, 141-145, 153-154
  bachelor, 134, 139-140, 144-145
  binary, 50-51, 133
  neutron, 73-74, 113-114, 120
  supergiant, 112-113, 117, 120
  variable, 13-14, 42-43
Static universe, 52-53
Statistical mechanics, 107-108
Steady state universe, 22-23, 59-63, 72, 84-85
Stellar ages, 134, 139-140, 143-144
Stellar colors, 139-140, 143-144
Stellar density, 119-121, 133-134, 139-140
Stellar location, 134, 139-140, 143-144
Stellar luminosity, 119, 134-135, 139-140, 143-144
Stellar masses, 117-119, 134, 139-140, 142-144
Strong anthropic principle (SAP), 128-129
Strong nuclear force, 68-69, 91, 111-113, 116-118
Sun, 40-41, 49-50, 57, 73-75, 116-117, 131-132, 134-138, 143-145, 147, 164

Supergiant stars, 112-113, 117, 120
Supernovae, 23-24, 73-75, 112-113,
        120, 132-133, 138-139,
        143-144
Super-time, 81-82
Surface gravity, 135-138, 139-140, 143-
        144

Tectonic plate activity, 135-138,
        140-142
Telescopes
    Hubble Space, 35-43, 45-46
    Keck, 45-46
    Mt. Wilson, 55
Temperature fluctuations, 23-29,
        32-33, 45-46, 84-85
Tensor calculus, 10-11
Thermodynamics, 15-16, 19-20, 49-50,
        65-66, 71, 109-110, 128
Tidal interaction, 134, 135-138, 139-
        140, 141-142, 143-144
Time, 72-73, 75-78, 79-84, 88-91,
        91-92, 96-98, 102-103, 107-108,
        111, 124-125, 147, 149-150,
        157-160
Timeless eternity, 83-84
Tornados, 135-138
Transcendent creation, 76-80, 130,
        157
Trinity, 77, 79-80, 157-160

Ultraviolet, 35-40
Ultraviolet radiation, 139-141,
        154-155
Unified field theory, 91-92, 158
Uniformity of the universe, 91-92,
        118-121
Unity, 79-80
Universe
    age of, 22-23, 42-43, 49-50, 58-61,
        117, 119, 150
    deceleration of, 42-43, 52

    expansion of, 42-46, 52, 53, 58-66,
        82-83, 116, 119
    homogeneity of, 91-92
    infinite, 49-50, 57, 60-61, 63-64, 71,
        106
    mass density of, 38-40, 42-43,
        63-65, 91-92, 119, 125
    multiple, 98-100, 123-126
    oscillating, 63-69, 71-72
    static, 52-53
    steady state, 22-23, 59-63, 72, 84-85
    uniformity, 91-92, 118-121

Vanadium, 112
Variable stars, 13-14, 42-43
Velocity of light, 31-32, 50-53,
        119
Venus, 134, 135-139, 154-155. *See also*
        Planets
Virtual particles, 96-97
Volcanos, 137, 140-141

Warm dark matter, 31-32
Watchmaker argument, 105-108,
        109-110
Water, 120, 135, 137, 139-141,
        154-155
Wave function, 89-90, 95
Weak anthropic principle (WAP),
        128-129
Weak nuclear force, 91, 111-113,
        116, 118
White dwarf binaries, 121, 133,
        138-140, 143-144

X-rays, 43-45, 154-155

Young-Earth creationists, 58, 81-82
Young galaxies, 44-45
Young stellar objects, 143-144
Young-universe creationism, 58

AUTHOR

HUGH ROSS earned a B.Sc. in physics from the University of British Columbia and an M.Sc. and Ph.D. in astronomy from the University of Toronto. For several years he continued his research on quasars and galaxies as a post-doctoral fellow at the California Institute of Technology. For eleven years he served as minister of evangelism at Sierra Madre Congregational Church.

Today he directs the efforts of Reasons To Believe, an institute founded to research and proclaim the factual basis for faith in God and in His Word, the Bible. He also hosts a weekly television series called "Reasons To Believe" on the Trinity Broadcasting Network. Over the years Hugh has given several hundred lectures, seminars, and courses, both in the United States and abroad, on Christian apologetics. He lives in Southern California with his wife, Kathy, and sons, Joel and David.

REASONS TO BELIEVE

REASONS TO BELIEVE is a nonprofit organization, without denominational affiliation, adhering to the doctrinal statements of the National Association of Evangelicals and of the International Council on Biblical Inerrancy. It provides research and teaching on the harmony of God's revelation in the words of the Bible and in the facts of nature. A hotline for those with questions or a desire to dialogue on issues pertaining to faith, science, and the Bible operates at (818)335-1480, Monday through Friday, 5-7 p.m, Pacific Time. A catalog of materials may be obtained by phoning the same number during office hours or by writing Reasons To Believe, P. O. Box 5978, Pasadena, CA 91117.

If you liked THE CREATOR AND THE COSMOS, be sure to check out these other books by Hugh Ross!

Creation and Time

Not all scientists disagree with the Bible about the age
of the earth. *Creation and Time* clearly explains how a divine
creation with long creation days resulting in an old earth is possible.

Creation and Time
(Hugh Ross) $12

Beyond the Cosmos

Scientific discoveries point to the existence of at least
eleven dimensions. This award-winning book explains what
these extra dimensions reveal about God and the incarnation,
atonement, free will, and predestination.

Beyond the Cosmos
(Hugh Ross) $20

Get your copies today at your local bookstore, or call
(800) 366-7788 and ask for offer **#2094**.

NAVPRESS
BRINGING TRUTH TO LIFE
www.navpress.com

Prices subject to change without notice.